INDIA AND AFRICA

Common Security Challenges for the Next Decade

INDIA AND AFRICA

Common Security Challenges for the Next Decade

Editor

Ruchita Beri

INSTITUTE FOR DEFENCE STUDIES & ANALYSES
NEW DELHI

PENTAGON PRESS

India and Africa: Common Security Challenges for the Next Decade
Editor: Ruchita Beri

First Published in 2016

ISBN 978-81-8274-860-6

Published by
PENTAGON PRESS
206, Peacock Lane, Shahpur Jat,
New Delhi-110049
Phones: 011-64706243, 26491568
Telefax: 011-26490600
email: rajan@pentagonpress.in
website: www.pentagonpress.in

Branch
Flat No.213, Athena-2,
Clover Acropolis,
Viman Nagar,
Pune-411014
Email: pentagonpresspune@gmail.com

In association with
Institute for Defence Studies and Analyses
No. 1, Development Enclave,
New Delhi-110010
Phone: +91-11-26717983
Website: www.idsa.in

Printed at Avantika Printers Private Limited.

Contents

Preface

Converging global security challenges over the coming decade, will necessitate combined efforts by states to manage threats and maximise opportunities. Among the most significant challenges that India and Africa will face in particular, are the reforms in global governance institutions, maritime security threats in the Indian Ocean, energy insecurity and the rise of extremism and terrorism. The last few decades have also seen a global power transition with the emergence of new powers such as China, India and Brazil. Africa, during this period has also witnessed a surge in economic growth and democratic governance. During this period of transition, India and Africa can jointly identify solutions for the critical common security challenges that face them both.

In recent years, fundamentalism has been on the rise in Africa. Several African countries are battling extremist groups that are clearly linked with Al-Qaeda and its affiliates. Nigeria has been involved in a war against Boko Haram for the past six years. A significant consequence of the Libyan crisis has been the strengthening of existing armed groups and the emergence of new extremist groups in West Africa. The Al-Shabaab group in Somalia is a known affiliate of Al-Qaeda and controls large swathes of the country. The rise of religious fundamentalism and the trans-national reach of these groups poses a threat not only to individual nations, but to regional and global security.

Maritime violence off the Horn of Africa has been the focus of global attention over the past decade or so, with piracy in the Indian Ocean region being the most prominent threat. Piracy linked with the internal instability in Somali has contributed most to the maritime insecurity in this region.

Of late, piracy off Somalia has reduced but it has increased in the Gulf of Guinea region. India and Africa have a common interest in securing this shared maritime space and cooperating to address these common concerns.

There has been an increasing recognition of the cross-cutting nature of security issues in the last decade. Global concerns such as climate change and energy security demand increased cooperation across national borders. Despite being well endowed with energy resources, Africa faces critical challenges in its energy sector, which is mainly characterised by lack of access, poor infrastructure, low purchasing power and low energy efficiency. These remain major obstacles to the achievement of full economic development. Meanwhile, India's ability to maintain its economic growth will be heavily influenced by how it manages its growing energy demands.

Against this backdrop, this book marks an effort to combine Indian and African perspectives on the common security challenges that they are likely to face in the foreseeable future. It has emerged from the papers presented at the Second India-Africa Strategic Dialogue organised by the Institute for Defence Studies and Analyses, New Delhi in November 2013. It also seeks answers to a wide spectrum of issues: What are the most important security challenges that India and Africa will face in the coming decade? Can India and the affected African states share the lessons derived from the transnational terrorist threats facing them both? What are the emerging threats to maritime security in India and Africa? What are the critical challenges that Africa and India face in the energy sector? How can both sides cooperate in resolving these challenges?

In Chapter 1 Francis Kornegay compares, contrasts and assesses areas of security cooperation convergence between India and Africa in the backdrop of the global security scenario. He identifies the geopolitical structural parameters of convergence and divergence between Africa and India. He argues that overcoming the embedded asymmetries between a fragmented Africa and the Indian sub-continental mega-state is critical from an African perspective. He highlights the need for a more comprehensive look at the range of non-traditional as well as traditional security threats along the Afro-South Asian axis.

In Chapter 2 Ruchita Beri examines the emerging India -Africa security engagement. It would be wrong to assume that Africa's insecurity is only an African problem. Africa's internal problems have repercussions beyond its natural borders; piracy in the Indian Ocean region being just one example of this malaise. Thus, it is imperative that each stakeholder, both inside and outside the continent, be involved in resolving these insecurity issues. India can be one such player. As India's engagement grows, the instability in the region may pose a threat to India's investments on the continent. Thus it will be fruitful to analyse India's role in addressing Africa's security challenges. Beri underscores India's support in training, peacekeeping and maritime security on the continent and examines its convergence with African countries on issues related to peacekeeping at the UN.

Festus Kofi Aubyn in Chapter 3 argues that terrorism/extremism are the most immediate challenges facing many countries in Africa. While there can be no doubt that the direct impact of terrorism and extremism on the continent is borne by the African states, its consequences for global security and bilateral partners who are strategically linked with this threat, cannot be underestimated. In particular, the established links between terrorist groups such as Al-Qaeda in South Asia and Al-Shabaab and the Al-Qaeda in the Islamic Maghreb (AQIM) in Africa make India, which is both a victim of terrorism and a member of SAARC, an important partner in the fight against the menace. Aubyn examines the initiatives and mechanisms evolved by African states and regional organisations for combating terrorism/ extremism and identifies some useful lessons that can be drawn from the Indian experience of dealing with terrorism. He concludes that terrorism is not just a military problem; it is also a social, economic, political and ideological problem. Therefore, a viable counter-terrorism strategy should not only focus on using hard power, but soft power as well.

Vivek Chadha highlights some of the important lessons learned by India with regard to terrorist threats and the policy and operational options for dealing with similar threats in Africa in Chapter 4. It is evident from these lessons that even as global best practices are useful for dealing with such threats, solutions need to have local moorings if they are to succeed in a specific environment. Chadha also emphasises the importance of building capacities over a period of time, while simultaneously displaying the political maturity required to address some of the challenges faced by both India and Africa.

In Chapter 5 Manish Chand maps out the spread of terrorism in Africa and the key terror/militant groups involved in it. He also identifies the root causes and the various socio-economic reasons for the spurt of terrorism in Africa, as well as the efforts made by African countries to counter the menace. He explores the ramifications of terrorism in Africa for global security and what it means for countries like India, who are scaling up their economic and energy ties with the African continent. Chand highlights the huge stakes India has in curbing terrorism in Africa and recommends the deepening of security and counter-terror cooperation between India and the African continent.

In Chapter 6 Alex Benkenstein notes that the escalation of maritime violence off the Horn of Africa during the first decade of the 21st century has been met by an unprecedented level of international political and military cooperation, that is indicative of the strategic importance of the Indian Ocean for numerous regional and global powers. While incidents of piracy have decreased in recent years, the attacks have also been marked by greater sophistication and a wider geographic reach. Moreover, the expansion of the energy resource sector in the West Indian Ocean will give rise to new challenges and enhance vulnerabilities with regard to regional maritime security in the coming decade. Benkenstein also provides an overview of the changing energy resources profile of the West Indian Ocean region and assesses the priorities for India-Africa maritime security cooperation in the coming decade.

In Chapter 7 Vijay Sakhuja warns that coastal spaces represent both promise and peril. At one end of the spectrum, they provide the muscle for economic growth and development, and on the other hand these spaces have the potential to become the focal points for illegal activities. Lack of governance and an ineffective security apparatus has created conditions that favour the rise of terrorism, piracy and other illegal activities. Further, terrorism 'from the sea' is a reality as demonstrated by the Mumbai terror attacks. Post the Mumbai terror attacks in 2008, India undertook a major overhaul of its coastal security apparatus and also initiated a dialogue with some of its maritime neighbours to counter transnational maritime threats and challenges. Sakhuja hopes that the Indian experience in this regard will enable African states to adopt best practices for enhancing their maritime security.

Over the past few years there has been a positive, albeit gradual, change in India's maritime outlook towards Africa argues Abhijit Singh in Chapter 8. In view of the increasing Indian economic engagement in the African continent, New Delhi has sought to expand its maritime operations in the Western Indian Ocean. This has in some instances led to maritime collaboration between India and East African states. The primary driver of India's African maritime security initiative has been piracy off the shores of Somalia. The Indian navy has significantly contributed to the anti-piracy operations in the far reaches of the Western Indian Ocean. There is, however, a realisation on India's part that in order to make a substantive contribution, maritime security engagement with Africa will need to go beyond 'piracy assistance' in Somalia and the security of the sea lines of communication (SLOCs) in the Eastern Indian Ocean. Singh argues that India's growing maritime influence, and Africa's rising expectations with regard to the commitment of partner states to regional maritime security efforts, leaves New Delhi with little option but to up its involvement in maritime security of coastal Africa.

Shebonti Ray Dadwal notes in Chapter 9 that as one of the largest energy consuming and importing countries in the world, energy security is critical for India's national security. Access to Africa's huge and growing resources is therefore, a major reason for enhancing its engagement with the continent, be it for purchasing hydrocarbons and/or uranium, or acquiring stakes in Africa's energy assets. On the other hand, Africa, despite being well endowed with resources, is one of the least "energised" continents in the world, with vast parts of the continent having no access to modern forms of energy. Moreover, the majority of African countries, even those that require more sustainable and cleaner forms of energy to combat climate change pressures, do not have adequate energy resources. She argues that given the long, historical linkages and growing economic ties between India and Africa, it is imperative that they work together to ensure a mutually beneficial relationship, in both the renewable and non-renewable energy sectors.

India's rapidly growing dependence on oil has prompted it to seek strategic resources on the African continent states Aparajita Biswas in Chapter 10. In choosing to establish relations with African oil-producing countries, India enjoys the advantage of engaging with comparatively new oil producing countries in the Gulf of Guinea and Sudan, which also offer significant investment opportunities. Biswas suggests that African countries are also benefiting from India's engagement. Its capacity-building programmes have made India an important player in the infrastructure (roads, railways, dams, power plants, etc.) sector. India has also undertaken pipeline projects, apart from helping to develop education and health facilities in many African countries.

Similarly Ambrose Ejiofor in Chapter 11, examines the major challenges facing Nigeria's oil and gas industry and how India and Nigeria can collaborate to tackle these challenges to their mutual benefit. With Nigeria dominating the prolific Gulf of Guinea as Africa's largest oil and gas producer, and accounting for over one-fifth of the continent's crude oil and gas production, any threat to energy supply from Nigeria will impact the African output. The implication is that as India is becoming increasingly dependent on Africa, particularly Nigeria for crude oil, any major energy challenge in Nigeria will have grave consequences for India. Ejiofor states that the development of Nigeria's energy sector is also being hampered by the lack of gas infrastructure required for harnessing the abundant gas resources, militancy, vandalism, crude oil theft, uncertainty of the operating environment following the non-passage of the Petroleum Industry Bill (PIB) and hostility of oil and gas-producing communities, among other factors.

Africa and India both need development, and for development, energy resources are indispensable notes Rajiv Nayan in Chapter 12. India is an energy deficient country, and is in search of energy both from conventional and non-conventional sources. Nuclear energy is an important element in India's potential energy mix. In fact, India is one of the primary propellants of the current phase of the nuclear renaissance. It is constructing six nuclear reactors and has plans to build at least 25 more. The current nuclear expansion plan requires uranium. After the 2008 Nuclear Suppliers Group (NSG) exemptions, India received uranium from three countries and now wants to diversify its uranium supply. Several studies indicate that Africa may emerge as a significant supplier of uranium. Therefore Nayan suggests that India should look upon Africa as an alternate supplier of uranium.

This volume would not have been possible without the cooperation of the Ministry of External Affairs, Government of India. I appreciate the support of Jayant Prasad, Director General, IDSA in this endeavour. Special thanks are due to Arvind Gupta, Deputy National Security Advisor, Government of India and former Director General, IDSA for his encouragement. I also thank Rumel Dahiya, Deputy Director General, IDSA. At the same I acknowledge the assistance provided by Nachiket Khadkiwala and Saurabh Mishra. Finally, I would like to thank Vivek Kaushik, Associate Editor, IDSA, Rajan Arya and Virender Negi of the Pentagon Press for bringing out this volume on time. It is hoped that the views expressed in this book will lead to a greater understanding of the common security challenges facing Africa and India.

Ruchita Beri

About the Editor/Contributors

Festus Kofi Aubyn is a Research Fellow at the Faculty of Academic Affairs and Research (FAAR) of the Kofi Annan International Peacekeeping Training Centre (KAIPTC) in Ghana and currently a doctoral candidate in Peace and Conflict Studies at the University of Ibadan, Nigeria. His research interests are in the areas of conflict, peace and security in Africa with a particular focus on peace operations; transnational organized crimes; election security. He has participated and presented papers in many local and international conferences on peace and security issues in Africa. Aubyn also has a number of publications to his credit. Among his recent publications (co-authored) are 'Ghana' in Alex J. Bellamy and Paul D. Williams (eds.), *Providing Peacekeepers: The Politics, Challenges and Future of UN Peacekeeping Contributions* (Oxford: Oxford University Press, 2013); 'Challenges in Mali: Historic duty to ensure peace' (*New Routes, 2013*) 'Unconstitutional Changes of Government: Confronting Africa's Democratic Paradox' (*AU Herald*, Vol. 3, 2013); 'Africa's Resistance to Peacekeeping's Normative Change' (*CSS ETH Zurich and GCSP Policy paper,* 2013); and 'China's Foray into African security and the Question of Non-interference' (*African East-Asian Affairs, Issue 03, 2013*).

Alex Benkenstein is a Senior Researcher for the South African Institute of International Affairs (SAIIA), where he forms part of the Governance of Africa's Resources Programme. His research focus at SAIIA has included co-management, resource-related conflict, ocean governance and climate change, with a particular emphasis on the mining and fisheries sectors. Previously he was employed by the consultancy Managing for Excellence, where he completed projects for various public and private sector clients, including the Parliament of South Africa. He was subsequently appointed as Head of Research for the NGO Regency Foundation Networx, where his work focused on private sector responses to emerging issues surrounding climate change.

Ruchita Beri is a Senior Research Associate and Coordinator, Africa, Latin America, Caribbean and United Nations Centre at the Institute for Defence Studies and Analyses (IDSA), New Delhi, specialising in political and security issues of Sub-Saharan Africa. Her current research focus is on India-Africa relations. She is the Vice President of the African Studies Association of India and an alumna of the Women in International Security (WIIS), USA. She is also the member of Africa Committee of the Confederation of Indian Industry (CII) and the Indian Council of World Affairs (ICWA). She has lectured at various Indian institutions including National Defence College, College of Naval Warfare, and Foreign Service Institute; and has participated in several international conferences. She is on the Editorial Board of *Austral: Brazilian Journal of Strategy & International Relations*. She has edited two books, *India and Africa: Enhancing Mutual Engagement (2014)*; *Africa and Energy Security (2009)* and has contributed journal articles and book chapters to over 80 publications.

Aparajita Biswas is a Professor at the Centre for African Studies, University of Mumbai. She completed her M.A. in International Relations from Jadavpur University, Kolkata (erstwhile Calcutta). She is associated with many universities, research institutes and research groups in India and abroad. She is the President of African Studies Association of India and the editor of the *Africa Review*, Journal, published by Routledge. Her main interest in research includes India- Africa relations, Africa's oil sector, Energy Security, Regional organizations in Asia and Africa, Africa and the Indian Ocean region and South and Southern Africa. Her articles have been published in many national and international journals. Her latest books are *India- Africa Enduring Partnership: Emerging Areas of Cooperation* (2013) and *India- East Africa: Security Relations* (2013), published from Nairobi University.

Vivek Chadha, is a Research Fellow at the IDSA. He has served in the army for 22 years, before joining IDSA in 2011. This included the command of a battalion on the Line of Control in Jammu and Kashmir (J&K) (2007-2008), Staff Officer to the Chief of Army Staff (2005-2007) and active service in counterinsurgency operations in Sri Lanka, Northeast India and J&K, prior to this. He was also involved with the writing of Indian Army's first Sub Conventional Doctrine (2006). He held the Maharana Pratap Chair (2002-2003) and Colonel Pyara Lal Memorial Scholarship (2005-2006), at The United Service Institution of India. He has authored a number of single author books which include: *Indo-US Relations: From Divergence to Convergence* (2007), *Low Intensity Conflicts in India: An Analysis* (2005)

Manish Chand is Editor-in-Chief of India Writes, a magazine and journal focused on international affairs, emerging powers, Africa and dialogue among cultures. He is also Managing Director of The Global Insights India (TGII), a media, publishing research and consultancy company. He has served as Editor of Africa Quarterly, a journal focused on African issues and India-Africa relations, published by the Indian Council for Cultural Relations (ICCR) for the last eight years. He is also a member of the Advisory Board on Africa for the Indian Council of World Affairs (ICWA). He is editor of *Two Billion Dreams: Celebrating India-Africa Friendship*, a book capturing myriad facets of India-Africa relationship. The book was launched at the second Africa-India Forum Summit in Addis Ababa in May 2011. He is a co-editor of "Engaging with Resurgent Africa" (McMillan) that explores different trajectories of engagement by emerging powers with the resurgent African continent.

Shebonti Ray Dadwal is a Research Fellow with the Institute for Defence Studies and Analyses, New Delhi, specializing on energy security and climate change-related issues. She has worked as Senior Editor in The Financial Express and she has also served as Deputy Secretary at the National Security Council Secretariat. She has presented papers in national and international conferences and has written several peer-reviewed articles and papers on her area of work. Ms. Dadwal was awarded the FCO Chevening Fellowship on The Economics of Energy in April 2009. In

2002, she published a book, *Rethinking Energy Security in India*, and is now working on the politics of energy and climate change.

Alike Ambrose Ejiofor is the Energy Correspondent of This Day Newspaper, Nigeria's most influential national daily. He has also worked for Business Day, Nigeria's number one business newspaper as Energy Analyst. He specialises in gathering, analysing, interpreting and reporting oil, gas and power supply issues with special focus on Nigeria. He has attended and participated actively in many oil and gas conferences. He attended the prestigious Lagos Business School, where he obtained a Certificate in Advanced Writing and Reporting Skills and the University of Nigeria, Nsukka, where he obtained a Bachelor of Science (B.Sc) degree in Accountancy and a Masters in Business Administration (MBA).

Francis A. Kornegay, Jr. is a Senior Fellow at the Institute for Global Dialogue, University of South Africa (UNISA) and a Global Fellow of the Smithsonian Woodrow Wilson International Center of Scholars (WWICS) in Washington, DC with which he is a member of its expert team on global governance. Kornegay twice served as a professional staffer in the US Congress where he drafted the last sanctions bill against apartheid South Africa. He also helped set up the Office of Research and Evaluation at the African Development Foundation and headed up the South African office of the African-American Institute in Johannesburg. Kornegay has played a major role in the annual BRICS think-tank symposia and academic forums and is a former columnist for *Business Day*. He is widely published on a variety of African and non-African global geopolitical and governance themes. He is lead co-editor of the, *Laying the BRICS of a New Global Order: From Yekaterinburg 2009 to eThekwini 2013* (Africa Institute of South Africa). Kornegay has also been active in IBSA research and academic dialogues and is currently focusing on oceans governance and maritime security issues pertaining to the Indian Ocean and the South Atlantic as well as writing a critical reflection monograph on America's foreign policy transition.

Rajiv Nayan is a Senior Research Associate at the Institute for Defence Studies and Analyses, New Delhi. He has been working with the Institute since 1993, where he specializes in export control, non-proliferation, and arms control. He was a Visiting Research Fellow at Japan Institute of International Affairs, Tokyo, where he published his monograph- Non-Proliferation Issues in South Asia. He was also a Senior Visiting Research Fellow at King's College London and a Visiting Fulbright Scholar at the Center on International Cooperation, New York University. He holds a Ph.D. and a Master of Philosophy in Disarmament Studies from Jawaharlal Nehru University, New Delhi. In his doctoral dissertation, he studied implications of the Missile Technology Control Regime for Indian security and economy. He has published his papers in academic journals, and as chapters of books. He is a member of the governing council of the International Export Controls Association, hosted by University of Georgia in Washington, DC, and a member of the Export Controls Experts Group and Multilateral Security Governance in Northeast Asia/North Pacific of the Council for Security Cooperation in Asia Pacific (CSCAP). He is an Indian partner of Fissile Materials Working Group (FMWG) which is a Washington-based group of Non-Governmental Organisations active on nuclear security. He was a Member, Regional Network of Strategic Studies Centers Weapons of Mass Destruction/Border Security Working Group. He was also on the Executive Council of the Indian Pugwash Society.

Vijay Sakhuja is Director at the National Maritime Foundation, New Delhi. He is also Visiting Senior Research Fellow, Institute of Southeast Asian Studies (ISEAS). A former Indian Navy officer, he has been on the research faculty of a number of think tanks in India. He is author of *Asian Maritime Power in the 21st Century: Strategic Transactions -China, India and Southeast Asia* (2011) and *Confidence Building from the Sea: An Indian Initiative* (2001), Singapore and a manuscript *Politico-Strategic Developments in the Arctic* is under preparation. Vijay Sakhuja is editor of *India Vietnam Strategic Partnership: Exploring Vistas for Expanded Cooperation* (2011) and *Reinvigorating IOR-ARC* (2011) and co-editor of *India Vietnam Relations: Expanding the Partnership in the 21st Century* (2013); *Change in Myanmar* (forthcoming 2013); *India and the European Union: Expanding the Strategic Partnership* (2012), *Fisheries Exploitation in the Indian Ocean: Threats and Opportunities* (2010), and *Nagapattinam to Suvarnadwipa: Reflections on Chola Naval Expeditions to Southeast Asia* (2009).

Abhijit Singh is a Research Fellow at the IDSA. Commissioned in the Executive Branch of the Indian Navy in July 1994, he is a specialist in Gunnery and Weapons Systems and has served onboard frontline ships. During his tenure with the Flag Officer Doctrines and Concepts in 2006, he was actively associated in the formulation and articulation of naval doctrines and operational concepts. As the Officer-in-Charge of the Indian Navy's History Division in 2008, he assisted the late Vice Admiral GM Hiranandani (Retd) in the authorship of the third volume of Indian Naval History, "Transition to Guardianship". Prior to joining the IDSA, he was a Research Fellow at the National Maritime Foundation (NMF) for three years where he researched and wrote extensively on Indian Ocean littoral security and geo-political events in West Asia and South Asia. At the IDSA, he has been looking at maritime security in the 'Indo-Pacific' Region. He has co-edited the book *Indian Ocean Challenges—a Quest for Cooperative Solutions* (2013).

1

Common Security Challenges for India and Africa: An overview

Francis A. Kornegay, Jr

Introduction

The global security environment in which India and Africa are situated reflects a complex interplay between the following multiplicity of trends: inter and intra-state tensions; conflicts and instabilities relating to regime legitimacy interacting with the increasing salience of non-state challengers to incumbent governments; regional geopolitical arrangements; shifting regional power balances between important and dominant state actors; the ongoing importance of access to energy and natural resources as requirements for economic growth in the global security calculus of major state actors; the closely interrelated growth of the oceanic maritime realm in energy security and commercial transport equations interacting with the emergence of threats to sea-going traffic; the global illicit economy involving illegal trafficking in drugs, arms and people, interacting with migratory cross-border population flows; the humanitarian security threat of natural disasters; challenges of expanding population growth and the pressures these exert on the scale and pace of economic growth and development and on the environment; and the threat of anthropogenic climate change interacting with these interrelated demographic-developmental pressures on environments.

The complexity of these multi-dimensional security challenges has to do with the comparatively diffuse nature of the global security environment interacting with regional variants and the fact that there are many other factors of a societal nature impacting on political stability in India and Africa. More fundamentally, this environment is shaped by insecurities arising out of the social, economic and technological forces propelling humanity's reintegration into an ever more interdependent and interconnected global community. In the process, virtually every aspect of human existence is being securitised.

In effect, what is being witnessed, in what I like to call the Age of Global Integration, is a phase of human evolution wherein the original out-of-Africa dispersal of humankind into far-flung communities which became distinct cultures and civilisations is currently being forced back together in a reintegrating process of cross-cultural and inter-civilisational interaction. Here, it is important to bear in mind that this re-integrative trend is unfolding against the backdrop of a projected population growth of 7 billion to 9 billion by 2050. The centre of gravity of this expansion embraces Africa and India in what amounts to a veritable Afro-South Asian demographic nexus.

The population of Africa, already at one billion is expected to reach two billion by 2050 while India is expected to overtake China, with both Africa and India having youthful rather than aging generational cohorts. From about 2050 to the end of this century, Asia and Africa, not counting the rest of the world, will have a combined population of 8 billion people with the global centre of gravity shifting to the Indian Ocean which constitutes a veritable 'Afro-Asian lake'. The main message to take away from this background is that the global evolutionary trend of human reintegration, with its demographic implications is shaping regional and interregional security environments.

Population growth pressures in Africa and India present security challenges to societal stability and national integration. The security concern here is in terms of how these pressures play out in rural-to-urban migration, the socio-cultural and governance adjustments demanded of such trends and how the coping capacities of cities to economically absorb growing numbers of people are impacted. Thus, as a shorthand definitional means of conceptualising such challenges, we might refer to them as *societal stability security challenges* (of human reintegration).

Basic social services are affected and implicated in governance challenges at all levels reflecting manifold human security imperatives: the need to meet the challenges of youth by prioritising education, training and job-creation along with youth development programmes; attention to grass-roots community economic development that is participatory and responsive; coming to terms with multi-dimensional gender inequalities while enhancing the security of women, including encouraging security initiatives to be undertaken by women themselves as a mobilisational complement to law enforcement and policing reforms.

All of these security-related issues, whether at the more macro-level of geopolitical, state-centric concerns relating to what might be termed the international relations of security, or at more localised levels having to do with societal stability, are shared in common by India and Africa, though in different contexts. Here, the contextual differences between the subcontinental mega-state India and a multi-state fragmented continental Africa are critical for understanding, what the two have in common and areas where security cooperation can be developed.

Indeed, this asymmetry between Africa and India and other external actors, both developed and emerging, requires a lot more elaboration for gaining a perspective on common security challenges. But, before elaborating further on this point, there is a need to review some more of the specificities of the general global security environment sketched out above. This is important for arriving at a more clearly resolved geopolitical-strategic linkage between India and Africa within the context of the global security environment.

The Strategic Landscape: Challenges facing India and Africa

The common security challenges facing India and Africa form part of the larger geopolitical landscape of connectivity in what might be considered an 'arc of upheaval.' This fraught geography ranges along the western Indian Ocean Rim (IOR) from the northeastern Horn of Africa into the

Maghreb and the Levant bordering the eastern Mediterranean into the southwest Asian Hindu Kush and the triple connectivity that joins Afghanistan, Pakistan and India.

Given the Mediterranean-Indian Ocean scope of this geography, maritime security issues are intimately interrelated with on-shore geopolitical dynamics and/or, as in the case of Somalia, are extensions of it. Otherwise, regional inter and intra-state dynamics animating security challenges converge in, and around the following trends:

- The emergence since, roughly the mid-1990s, of a Sunni jihadist terror threat evolving as a 'blow back' phenomenon out of the anti-Soviet war in Afghanistan accompanying Indo-Pakistani conflict over Kashmir while establishing African roots in the Tanzania-Kenya-Somali nexus and in Sudan as prelude to extending into the Maghreb. This matrix tracks the emergence of Al-Qaeda which has spawned something of a franchise network of Al-Qaeda in the Maghreb (AQIM) and Al-Qaeda in Arabian Peninsula (AQAP) and the affiliated Somali al-Shabaab. This sectarian terrorist threat intersects with more traditionally nationalist oppositional movements in Palestine and Lebanon. As such, the 'terrorist' label that some attach to Hamas and Hezbollah would seem to be highly debatable and politically inspired within the context of mideast sectarian geopolitics.
- Intra-state challenges to incumbent governments throughout this geography indicate a protracted era of disintegrative statelessness consuming the Somali Coast and its fragmentation into autonomous units; sectional warfare in Sudan leading to the breakaway establishment of an unstable South Sudan and a continuing post-independence conflict between the Sudans as well as the unresolved conflict within and between Darfur and Khartoum; post-Qaddafi challenges to the cohesion of Libya spilling over into a wider swathe of instability in the Sahel (Mali) and the Maghreb reinforced by the stalemated 'frozen conflict' in Western Sahara and merging into the terrorist challenge posed by AQIM. This pattern of intra-state instability with regional spillover potential extends into the northern tier of the Middle East in the Syrian civil war; the perennial Kurdish

question; virtual sectarian civil war in post-occupation Iraq; the Baluch resistance in Pakistan and the Naxalite Maoist insurgency spanning India's eastern states merging into tensions along India's borders with Bangladesh and Myanmar in addition to inter/intra-state tensions between India and Pakistan over Kashmir.

- An additional layer of inter/intra-state dynamics has been injected by the Arab Spring instabilities leading to unsettled transitions in Tunisia, Libya and Egypt complicated by the re-emergence of jihadist forces who initially appeared to have been placed on the 'back-foot' by what started out as an incipient transnational democratic revolution. Counterrevolutionary reaction to the Arab Spring among the Persian Gulf monarchies merging into sectarian geopolitical manoeuvring between the House of Saud and Iran has greatly propelled the Arab Spring transitions into what, at best, are uncertain futures, thereby exacerbating regional insecurity.

Within this Afro-Asian 'arch of upheaval' are increasingly pronounced regional balance of power shifts. These shifts, on the one hand, are linked to intra-state dynamics currently powered by the Arab Spring and reactions to it on top of older fault lines. On the other hand, they emanate out of the US-led invasion of Iraq which destroyed the regional Sunni-Shia balance of power in Iran's favour, adding fuel to the fire of already existing intra-Islamic contradictions in what, by now can be conceptualised as a Global Islamic Civil War.[1]

These shifting balances in forces are fuelling conflicts and complicating security challenges throughout the Middle East and North Africa, into the Hindu Kush and South Asia. The interconnected prospect of a US-Russian settlement of the Syrian conflict redirecting the focus away from Assad incumbency toward the jihadist threat and a settlement of Iran's nuclear issues promises a realignment in the international politics of Western Asia which has already destabilised long term alliances, such as those between the US, Israel and Saudi Arabia with security implications for both India and Africa.[2] *Indeed, this logic seems to support closer African and Indian alignment with Tehran, given Riyad's financing of 'Salafist Wahabist' extremism.*

Based on the foregoing, inter and intra-state turbulence throughout the 'arc of upheaval' interacting with regional and interregional power shifts determines the terrain for examining the following themes of this conference in further detail:

- The rise of terrorism/extremism
- Maritime security challenges
- Emerging energy challenges in India and Africa
- Discerning common solutions to common problems

These themes, however, should be treated as points-of-departures for other dimensions, which could serve as sub-themes and/or themes in themselves interrelated to terrorism/extremism, maritime security and energy challenges. These relate to:

- Governance viability interacting with issues of sovereignty and integration
- Societal stability security challenges
- Environmental security for ecological sustainability

Although the foregoing panoramic survey of security challenges has been linked to the interregional strategic landscape associated with those regions of Africa that are contiguous to western Asia leading into India, the whole of the African continent is relevant to this discussion, in as much as all of Africa is covered in this dialogue. The irredentist and jihadist threat to Mali's stability and territorial integrity in the aftermath of the ouster of Muammar al-Qaddafi in Libya and the emergence of Boko Haram as a major security threat in northern Nigeria as well as the ongoing piracy threat in the Gulf of Guinea are indicative of the relevance of these themes throughout a much wider expanse of Africa, bringing the Atlantic Basin into play.

Against the geostrategic landscape of important security challenges confronting India and Africa, the issue of global governance reform takes on a degree of urgency amid little likelihood that such reform will be forthcoming any time soon. As such, what are the prospects for reform and how can Africa and India jointly and separately advance the agenda-setting momentum? Any attempt at answering this question relates intimately to how India and Africa can work towards institutionalising their security cooperation frameworks as it would appear that an interplay between such frameworks and global governance security reform would be required.

The Global Governance Conundrum

India and Africa share a common aspirational desire for global governance reform in multiple security sectors, focusing especially on the United Nations Security Council. More generally, this security conundrum is intimately interlinked with the governance conundrum at all levels: global, continental and regional, national and intra-state. However, at the global level, within the framework of the UN Security Council and its mandated peacekeeping and stabilisation missions in Africa, India already has a long history as a major troop contributor in any number of conflict situations. Increasingly, UN missions have become intertwined with the African Union (AU) peace and security agenda wherein hybrid UN-AU missions such as in Darfur or UN-backed AU missions such as AMISOM in Somalia have become the staple of current engagements.

The support India has given to AMISOM in particular is emblematic of the kind of security assistance and cooperation that it is engaged in within the Africa-India Forum summit framework. Delhi's commitment to contributing $2 million to AMISOM at the May 24, 2011 summit in Ethiopia falls squarely within India's geostrategic 'arc of turbulence' national security interest. But apart from such assistance, there are larger issues that Africa and India need to jointly focus on in regard to the issue of UN Security Council reform. This has to do with the institutional as well as political capacity of the UNSC and other UN machinery to address Africa security challenges—and for that matter, similar challenges in South Asia as well.

The boilerplate focus on UNSC expansion has become such an obligatory item in communiqué after communiqué that a much deeper and broader reform substance has yet to be addressed. These might be illustratively identified as issues having to do with:

- whether or not the traditional peacekeeping rationale of mandated missions is still relevant;

- whether there may need to be an actual restructuring of the Security Council beyond adding new permanent members with implications for how the veto is employed;
- how the Security Council interacts with regional and continental peace and security institutions in a more federally structured manner of 'subsidiarity' which recognises continental and regional imperatives as paramount in deciding on missions to be mandated and undertaken and how implementation should unfold;
- the need for a restructuring of the UN's development machinery to better accommodate post-conflict reconstruction and recovery on a long-term basis linked to ongoing regional economic integration agendas.

These considerations should all be seen as being intimately interrelated with a more substantive UN peace and security stabilisation agenda that goes well beyond the boilerplate discourse on UNSC reform and traditional notions of 'peacekeeping;' but are out of context of where 'peacekeeping' appears increasingly to be headed: in the direction of comprehensive stabilisation.[3]

A needed transition: from 'peacekeeping' to 'stabilisation'

Why so? Because peacekeeping missions are becoming 'stabilisation' missions in implicit acknowledgement of the questionable capacity of many states to actually exist as sustainably sovereign entities as they emerge from conflict. This is reinforced by the possibility that this is/was the source of their conflict and endemic instability in the first place.

In a sense such situations could justify a veritable backtracking from independence back into forms of 'trusteeship' and so-called 'transitions to independence' (or 'democracy') that were much too short but where their propulsion into 'sovereignty' resulted from diplomatic and geopolitical compulsions that defied more cautious and deliberate preparations for sustainable governance. As 2013 drew to a close the conflict crisis situations that were spinning out of control in the Central African Republic (CAR) and in South Sudan were only the latest instances underlining this point.

An illustrative UN peace and security stabilisation reform (as opposed to purely UNSC reform) agenda might reflect the following elements:

- An expansion of the UNSC wherein new permanent members would be without the veto which would remain with the P5 but would be offset by an additional structure added to the Security Council in the form of a 'regional consultative forum' where regional and continental bodies like the EU, the AU, the soon to be ASEAN Community, NATO, the Collective Security Treaty Organisation (CSTO), the Shanghai Cooperation Organisation and the South American Defence Council would be represented and would not only have to be consulted but, with respect to their regional and/or continental domain, could override a P5 veto or exercise their own veto so as to assert 'regional autonomy' in determining missions to be mandated and how they would be implemented. In other words: a UN Security Council & Regional Consultative Forum (UNSC-RCF).
- Operationally and closely related to the forgoing, the actual 'hybridity' of UN/AU missions such as in the case of Darfur and AMISOM could serve as points-of-departure for elaborating a stabilisation strategy reflecting principles of 'subsidiarity' and 'regional autonomy' so that on-the-ground peace and security initiatives are not encumbered or held hostage to the sometimes convoluted diplomatic politics of the UNSC (although there may be ample politico-diplomatic convolutions unfolding at regional and continental levels as well!).
- Consideration might be given to consolidating the UNDP, the UN Peace-Building Commission, UNHCR and UNICEF into a UN 'development and stabilisation administration' or UNDSA wherein peacekeeping would be subsumed as one element under what are already emerging as 'stabilization missions' which, in turn, would be 'decentralised' (in terms of 'subsidiarity' and 'autonomy') via partnerships with regional and/or continental bodies (i.e. AU, NATO, CSTO, SCO, ASEAN, SAARC).[4]

Deepening UNSC reform

The point of these illustrative proposals is to emphasise the need for some creative 'thinking outside the box' in proactive India-Africa strategic cooperation on the issue of UN and global governance reform in advancing a common security agenda. Any serious momentum generated for advancing UN Security Council reform must factor in a more clearly resolved devolutionary role for continental governing bodies and regional economic communities in a more globally integrated sustainable security system.

What is implied here is the need for a more structured consultative role for continental and regional bodies in UNSC decision-making. This is needed, both as a reality-checking counterpoint and as a backstop to the P5 and any contemplated expansion of the permanent members. Hence, the idea of an institutional expansion of the UNSC to accommodate a 'regional consultative forum.' Such a vehicle would introduce another dimension sorely in need of being institutionalised into a reformed UN security system: the principles of 'devolution' and 'subsidiarity' applied to addressing local and regional specificities of the conflict prevention-management-resolution and post-conflict recovery stabilization chain in regard to particular crises.

Obviously, much more critical scrutiny and deliberation over such options are in order but are urgently needed, given the centrality of the UN to promoting global sustainable security. Yet, the UN should not be the only focal point of global security governance reform efforts. Rather, it should serve as the centrepiece of a more globally federalised order institutionalising devolutionary subsidiarity. Thus, there are other arenas of endeavour within the still fledgling context of 'south multilateralism' and the thinking through of alternative institutional security cooperation frameworks in need of attention.

Alternative Forms of Multilateral Cooperation and Institutional Frameworks

Global governance reform revolving around the UN naturally feeds into areas that have to do with issues of multilateralism and how Africa and India can work together in such a context. Multilateralism, however, has proliferated into a diversity of plurilateral and minilateral platforms beyond the traditional realms of the UN, the Non-Aligned Movement and the G77 (currently mutated into the G77+China) where Indian and African diplomacies used to focus. Multilateralism now has to factor in the 'club governance' terrain of the G20 where South Africa and India are both members while also holding memberships in IBSA, BRICS, BASIC and more functionalist organisations like the Indian Ocean Rim Association (formerly the Indian Ocean Rim-Association for Regional Cooperation).

Individually and jointly, within the framework of the Africa-India Forum, it might be useful for these two to conduct an 'audit' on how they should proceed in collaborating at these various levels and where priorities should focus. There are platforms in need of upgrading and reinvigorating such as the Indian Ocean Rim Association (IORA) as well as regional economic communities (RECs) operating at lower than necessary profiles like the South Asian Association for Regional Cooperation (SAARC) which could usefully partner in any number of endeavours with the ASEAN in South East Asia and the COMESA-SADC-EAC tripartite mega-trade initiative in Africa. In this regard, the recommendation that emerged in the conference discussion *that the AU become an observer member of the SAARC* as is the case with the EU should be acted on as a matter of urgency.

Why such RECs and interregional functionalist structures need greater attention in up-scaling their multilateral roles, has to do with the growing importance of regional and interregional integration. Here, one may venture that the most productive means of advancing common security is through advancing integration processes in Africa and Asia accompanied by strategic partnership networking between Asian and African RECs and regional organisations and initiatives, in effect, building an Afro-Asian security community within the Indian Ocean Rim.

How can this relate to climate change and counterterrorism? Here, there are two platforms in need of mention: one which has not received nearly the attention it deserves—the *New Asia Africa Strategic Partnership* (NAASP)—and BASIC, addressing ongoing climate change talks.

NAASP and the elusive Afro-Asian strategic partnership equation

From an African perspective, the NAASP, in particular needs serious revisiting within the context of Africa's relations not only with India but with China and other Asian actors as well. This is especially so given the very candid and appropriate criticism levelled by Ambassador Rajiv Bhatia that, thus far, the burden of the India-Africa strategic dialogue has been one-sidedly shouldered by India at the expense of a genuinely two-way conversation. The reason for this, which seems not to be adequately understood, is the asymmetry embedded in the structure of Africa's international relations with emerging powers and developed countries alike.[5]

The NAASP, launched as a joint Indonesia-South African Bandung revival initiative in 2005 has yet to live up to its initial promise as an Afro-Asian vehicle for strategic multilateral cooperation.[6] It has been grossly overshadowed by *bi-multilateral 'one and the many' initiatives* between Africa's 54 states and emerging Asian powers like India within the Africa-India Forum, FOCAC involving China, TICAD involving Japan, Brazil via the Lusophone geocultural grouping and now Turkey among others.

Africa's fragmentation condemns it to an embedded neocolonial relationship with all powerful external actors pursuing their national interest while oblivious to a predicament that puts Africa in a constant reactive mode. The NAASP, potentially could strengthen Africa's capacity to coordinate these diverse Asian bi-multilaterals. It is currently being integrated into the machinery of the AU, hopefully as an adjunct to the New Partnership for Africa's Development (NEPAD).

Given the AU's multifaceted agenda, it remains to be seen how it integrates the NAASP. Will it be integrated in a manner that helps the continent overcome it's fragmented 'one and the many' disadvantage in engaging Asian powers like India, factoring in the Africa-India Forum? Indeed, the NAASP may need to be reviewed in terms of a more focused agenda of multilateral cooperation being developed wherein certain areas falling within the broad scope of climate change and maritime security might be explored.

For example, there is a need for focused attention on environmental security in both Asia and Africa, wherein the biota of vast portions of both continents are under constant and growing threat from commercial initiatives involving external partners and from activities such as illicit logging, poaching and trafficking in wildlife and wildlife products along with off-shore fisheries depletion. In this regard, China and South East Asia have emerged as major global ecological threats to biodiversity.

Perhaps within the scope of the Reducing Emissions from Deforestation and Forest Degradation (REDD) initiative for addressing deforestation, there could be scope for the Africa-India Forum to carve out a complementary NAASP-BASIC agenda that forcefully addresses securing biodiversity as a corollary to the initiatives that emerged from the 2011 forum summit in Addis addressing agricultural development and related institutional capacity-building. This can extend into certain functional cooperation areas of environmental security in conserving marine resources under the IORA agenda as well.

The suggestion that India work with the AU to develop the NAASP as the chief *multilateral interface* for coordinating different Asian agendas on the continent was not seen by some Indian conference participants to be in India's national interest (for the kneejerk fear that this might eclipse the Africa-India Forum). However, it is definitely in Africa's continental interest to pursue such a course.

From the AU's vantage point, this would include developing the NAASP into an interfacing vehicle for coordinating relations with the FOCAC, TICAD and other such bi-multilateral initiatives, including the Africa-India Forum. Africa needs to better position itself to overcome its fragmentation in *proactively* navigating different Asian strategic partnerships. That should be what the NAASP is for. This might address Ambassador Bhatia's very well placed concerns about developing a more balanced two-way Indo-African conversation as opposed to 'one hand clapping.'

BASIC

The other forum involving the minilateral Brazil-South Africa-India-China—BASIC—platform for coordinating policy and strategy in climate talks raises other issues. Wherein South Africa is Africa's proxy within BASIC, a sort of 'agree to disagree' arrangement has evolved wherein the African agenda has tended to contradict the strategies of China and especially India, which has taken the toughest line on issues having to do with the legally non-binding nature of climate talk outcomes. In alignment with the rest of the continent, South Africa came out in favour of a legally binding follow up to the Kyoto Protocol.

To some extent, the more recent bilateral climate synergy between the US and China has brought about greater convergence in this regard. Otherwise, there should be room for Afro-Indian coordination on climate-related issues in terms of knowledge and technology sharing in functional areas of South-South cooperation. Here again, there may also be room for South Africa and the AU to coordinate synergies in climate diplomacy between the NAASP and BASIC in a manner that complements the Africa-India Forum agenda on such issues.

Conclusion

In effect, India-Africa cooperation within multilateral platforms will have to contemplate more proactive strategies for institutionalising such frameworks. This is especially urgent on the African side. More generally, the problem confronting South multilateralism overall is its inadequate institutionalisation. This affects the North-South balance overall. What remains is North-South asymmetry. This can only be redressed by creating a global South architecture. An excellent example in this regard has to do with the IBSAMAR naval initiative of India, Brazil and South Africa.

Here, India-Africa cooperation in the area of maritime security and functional cooperation could benefit from an IBSA decision to build upon the IBSAMAR initiative for elaborating a 'southern oceans governance architecture' through the commencing of a dialogue aimed at structuring such a framework. This is something that could contribute to informing IBSA's outreach with countries active in the Zone of Peace and Cooperation in the South Atlantic (ZPCSA) like Angola as well as those active in the IORA such as Indonesia and Australia. Iran should likewise be factored into this mix.

The fact that India's main national interest targets the Indian Ocean where it is geostrategically central should not detract from the need for a broader southern hemispheric multilateral subsystem. Such a system should link the Indian Ocean with the South Atlantic where South Africa is pivotal in its positioning astride the sea lanes between these bodies of water.[7] Embarking on the developing of such a linkage should help build leverage for propelling UN Security Council reform by introducing into the global security equation an important subsystem of multilateral cooperation. It would also reinforce a much needed devolutionary trend toward 'subsidiarity' in addressing common global security challenges, including those shared by both India and Africa.

For Africa and India, it is not enough to continually push for the need for UNSC and more general UN and global governance reform. To make such reform more compelling in building momentum, there is a need to proactively table comprehensive reform proposals and, where there is an opportunity as in the southern oceans, take action in making them a reality—'creating facts on the ground' so to speak. Given how demographically and commercially central the Indian Ocean is becoming, Africa and India have a major common security concern in oceanic community building in the southern hemisphere. This, in turn, will further the elaborating of a much needed southern hemispheric international subsystem to balance that existing in the global North.

NOTES

1. This conceptualization is to be found in *Somaliland: An African struggle for nationhood and international recognition*, by Iqbal D. Jhazbhay. Johannesburg & Pretoria, Institute for Global Dialogue & South African Institute for International Affairs, 2009. p. 243. See especially: "The geopolitics of the War on Terror and the Global Islamic Civil War," pp. 123-128 in Chapter 3 on "Religion (Islam)."
2. See for example, an anti-Barack Obama administration critique by Robert M. Cutler, "Washington's 'Fashoda' moment: The US reversal of alliances: Comparative perspectives," Asia Times Online, December 23, 2013. http://www.atimes.com/atimes/Middle_East/MID-04-231213.html. (Accessed on January 10, 2014)
3. For a discussion of stabilization, see: *Africa and Developmental Diplomacy in the Global South: The challenge of stabilization*. Pretoria, Africa Institute of South Africa (AISA), 2013, p. 42. Occasional paper no. 16 funded by the Open Society Foundation as part of the IGD project on South-South Cooperation.
4. Ibid., p. 22: "Towards a UN Development and Stabilization initiative."
5. For a discussion of the challenge this asymmetry presents to Africa in navigating relations with emerging powers see: "Engaging Emerging Powers: Africa's Search for a 'Common Position," by Francis A. Kornegay, Jr. & Chris Landsberg in *Politikon*, April 2009, pp. 171-191.
6. Francis A. Kornegay, Jr. *Pax-Afroasiatica? Revisiting Bandung Amid a Changing World Order*, Institute for Global Dialogue, 2004. Occasional paper. Also, more recently: "Pax-Afroasiatica and Bandung Revisited: From 1955-2005," in *Africa and Developmental Diplomacy in the Global South*, AISA occasional paper no. 16, 2013, pp. 5-9.
7. See the following published works by Francis A. Kornegay, Jr: *South Africa, The Indian Ocean and the IBSA-BRICS Equation: Reflections on Geopolitical and Strategic Dimensions*, ORF Occasional Paper #30, December 2011, p. 22. and "South Africa, the South Atlantic and the IBSA-BRICS Equation: The Transatlantic Space in Transition," *AUSTRAL: The*

Brazilian Journal of Strategy and International Relations, 2(3), 2013, pp. 75-100. Forging a dialogue linkage between Indian Ocean and South Atlantic stakeholders on issues of maritime security, functional cooperation and oceans governance is being launched as an Institute for Global Dialogue, University of South Africa project funded by the South African Foreign Policy Initiative of the Open Society Foundations in 2014.

2

India-Africa Security Engagement

Ruchita Beri

India's contact with African countries can be traced back to ancient times and in the post-independence period they have to a large extent been focused on enhancing political and economic relations. India's security relations with Africa have centred on providing training to African security personnel, participation in United Nations peacekeeping efforts in the region and maritime cooperation. In 2008 India initiated a new phase in its relations with the continent by hosting the first India Africa Forum Summit. This summit evolved a framework for India- Africa cooperation in several fields including peace and security related issues. The paper examines the emerging security engagement between India and Africa.

The African Security Environment

In recent years the African continent has witnessed some positive developments. This is evident from the rapid economic growth in the region. According to the *Economist*, Africa has been the fastest growing region in the world during the last decade with an average annual growth rate of five percent.[1] As a result Africa has moved from being perceived as a "hopeless continent" to a region that is on the rise. However this transformation may not last for long if efforts are not made to check the never ending cycle of conflicts in the region. Over the past 50 years more than half the African states, have been ravaged by conflict, at one time or another. While there has been considerable decline in interstate wars, intra-state conflicts are on the rise. Another important trend is that the conflicts are not only between the state and the non- state actors, but conflicts between non- state actors are also on the rise. This trend is visible in Somalia and the Democratic Republic of Congo. Other African countries such as Tunisia, Libya, Egypt, Sudan, South Sudan, the Ivory Coast and the Central African Republic have also been prone to conflict in recent years. At the same time an arc of instability across the continent, with terror groups, such as the Boko Haram in Nigeria, Al Qaeda in Islamic Maghreb (AQIM), the Movement for Unity and Jihad in West Africa (Mujao), Signed in Blood Battalion, Islamic Movement for Azawad (IMI) in Mali and the Al Shabab in Somalia, crafting chaos in the region. The upsurge of piracy in Indian Ocean littoral states in East Africa and the Gulf of Guinea region in West Africa has exacerbated the insecurity in the region.

The enduring nature of African conflicts may be due to multiple factors such as poor governance, the incomplete process of state building, corruption, and struggle for control of resources. While African countries, made several attempts to strengthen security through the Organisation of African Unity (OAU), it was the failure of the international community to respond effectively during the Somali crisis and the genocide in Rwanda in the 1990s that prompted the African leaders to evolve "African solutions for African problems". These enhanced efforts led to the transformation of the OAU into the African Union in 2002 and the emergence of the African Peace and Security Architecture (APSA). Notably, the African Union marks a change from the policy of non-interference as prescribed by the OAU, to one of non- indifference that calls for intervention in cases of genocide and ethnic cleansing. Recently as part of its 50th anniversary celebrations, the African Union pledged to silence guns by 2020.

Training and Peace Keeping

In this backdrop, what are the main features of India's security engagement with Africa? First, to a large extent the focus has been on imparting training to the armed forces officers from various African countries. The Indian defence forces have the unique experience of operating in various terrains and also have the finest training facilities for jungle, desert and snow warfare. Over the years India has trained several military officers from African countries at the military training institutions within India such as the Indian Military Academy, Defence Staff College and the National Defence College. Some of the prominent alumni include, the current President Muhammadu Buhari as well as the former Presidents Ibrahim Babangida, Olusgun Obasanjo from Nigeria and Fred Akkufo, the former President of Ghana. It has also been involved in training and infrastructure development in countries such as Ethiopia, Nigeria, Mauritius, Zambia, Ghana, Sudan, Botswana, South Africa, Tanzania, Egypt and Lesotho. This entailed the building of operational and administrative facilities and infrastructure such as roads, airfields, communication networks etc. One of the first training institutions set up with Indian help in Africa was the Haile Selassie Harar military academy in Ethiopia in the year 1958. This academy not only trained military officers from within Ethiopia but also from several other African countries. Historical developments led to the closure of the academy in 1977. It was also involved in the establishment of National Defence College of Nigeria and Ghana. Indian officers were initially deployed as trainers in both these countries. At present, India continues to help African countries to enhance their capacities to train their military personnel.

India is also involved in stabilising the security situation on the African continent through active participation in the United Nations Peacekeeping Operations (UNPKO). While India's contribution to the UN peacekeeping budget may be less than one percent, it has contributed nearly 160,000 troops, the largest by any country, for 43 UN peacekeeping missions across the world.[2] As around 70 percent of UN peacekeepers worldwide, and more than 50 percent of the UN peacekeeping missions in the post Cold War era have been deployed in Africa, it can be argued that to a large extent Indian peacekeepers have been involved in reducing conflict in this troubled region.[3] India has participated in most of the UN peacekeeping missions in the continent, beginning with the Congo (1960-64). Subsequently India participated in missions to: Namibia (1989-90); Angola (1989-1995); Mozambique (1992-94); Somalia (1991-94); Rwanda (1993-

96); Sierra Leone (1999-2001); and Ethiopia-Eritrea (2006-08). Currently Indian peacekeepers are deployed in UN peacekeeping missions in: Liberia (since April 2007), Ivory Coast (since April 2004), the Democratic Republic of Congo (since January 2005) and Sudan/South Sudan (April 2005 onwards). Moreover, Indians have been involved in leadership roles as force commanders, police commissioners, military and police advisers in various UN Missions.

However in the post-Cold War era the United Nations peacekeeping operations in the Africa region have become extremely complex. Much of this has to do with the changing nature of warfare. Most of the ongoing conflicts in Africa occur within the countries rather than between them. These intra-state conflicts affected not just the combatants but also the civilians and had a disastrous impact on the economy and socio-economic fabric of the entire region. Another feature of these new generation conflicts is that they are quite unpredictable and intractable. Most often the blue helmets were deployed in areas where there was no peace to keep. Low intensity warfare accompanied peace agreements. Hence the traditional form of peacekeeping proved ineffective in dealing with the realities on the ground. Over the years UN peacekeeping operations have come to include peacebuilding; that requires vast civil military activity as well as peace enforcement that authorises use of force under Chapter VII of the UN charter. A turning point in peacekeeping mission mandates was starkly visible in the new force that was approved earlier this year for deployment in the Democratic Republic of Congo (DRC). After 14 years of peacekeeping in the DRC, the UN has now deployed a new kind of offensive force, an "Intervention Brigade", primarily to break the cycle of violence and disarm the rebels. This represents the most robust mandate ever given to UN peacekeepers to end conflict. Moreover, ambitious Security Council mandates tasked peacekeepers with a set of duties that ranged from early economic recovery to election monitoring, but the mandates were not matched by the resources required to fulfil them and there was a disconnect between the demands made on the peacekeepers and their ability to perform these tasks.

India has expressed its concerns over some of these new trends in peacekeeping and has raised the issue during debates on UN peacekeeping during its tenure as a non-permanent member of the Security Council from 2011 to 2012 and even subsequently.[4] First it has called for a greater role for troop contributing countries in the process of decision making and the shaping of the peacekeeping mandates. India has vociferously argued for the implementation of Article 44 of the United Nations Charter that calls upon the Security Council to invite the troop contributing states that are not members of the Council to participate in drawing up the peace keeping mandates.[5] This viewpoint is acceptable to countries in Africa as increasingly countries, such as, Egypt, Ghana, Kenya, Malawi, Niger, Nigeria, Rwanda, Senegal, Tanzania, Uganda, Zambia and Zimbabwe are contributing troops for the UN peacekeeping missions. India has also flagged the issue of the "severe mismatch between resources and ambitious mandates of peacekeeping operations".[6] This was with particular reference to the multi-dimensional peacekeeping mission in Central African Republic. India has also supported African countries in their push for greater synergy between the UN and the AU. During an open debate on peacekeeping operations in the Council, India also called for the strengthening of cooperation between the United Nations and African Union to ensure the effectiveness of peacekeeping operations and sought? Greater financial support for UN authorised AU peacekeeping operations.

There is a convergence in the perspectives of Indian and African countries in the peacekeeping debate except for India's concerns relating to the mixing of the traditional peace keeping mandate of the United Nations with the new robust interventionist mandate, for a small section of troops in the same peacekeeping operation in the United Nations Organisation Stabilization Mission in the Democratic Republic of Congo (MUNUSCO). In India's view such a mixed mandate exposes the UN peacekeepers to dangers in the armed conflict. Moreover all UN peacekeepers and not just those in the interventionist brigade will be liable to be treated as enemy combatants under international law and may also lose their impartiality. African countries on the other hand, have welcomed this move and have appreciated the success of the interventionist brigade in neutralising the M23 rebels in Congo.

Apart from providing support to African countries at a multilateral forum such as the UN, India has bilaterally been supportive of the African Union's efforts for enhancing the region's peace and security architecture. In this context India has pledged one million dollars for the African led

Support Mission in Mali, and two million dollars for the African Union Mission in Somalia (AMISOM).[7] India's interest in supporting AU initiatives is also visible in the regular presence of high ranking Indian officials at the AU summits. India's Vice President Hamid Ansari represented India during the 50th anniversary AU summit in Addis Ababa in 2013.[8]

Maritime Cooperation

In recent years India has also taken the initiative to provide maritime security in its strategic neighbourhood. It has committed to improving the maritime environment in the Indian Ocean region by becoming the "net security provider".[9] In this context it has forged security relations with Indian Ocean littoral states in Africa such as Mozambique, Mauritius and the Seychelles. Since 2000, India has been jointly patrolling the Mauritius EEZ along with the Mauritian coastguard. It has over the years provided several weapon systems such as seaward defence boats, interceptor patrol boats, aircraft, helicopters and an offshore patrol vessel, to Mauritius. The Indian navy also carries out hydrographic surveys in the country and transferred a hydrographic survey vessel to Mauritius in 2013. India also assists the Seychelles by undertaking maritime surveillance and providing military equipment. It has transferred a fast attack vessel, an aircraft and helicopters to the island nation.

During Prime Minister Narendra Modi's visit to these two island states in March 2015, India signed pacts to strengthen relations with these two countries. It has agreed to help build sea and air transport facilities in the Agalega Island (Outer Island) in Mauritius. This will go a long way towards helping the Mauritian defence forces to protect their interests in the Outer Island.[10] Similarly in the Seychelles Prime Minister Modi inked a pact to develop infrastructure in the Assumption Island and also inaugurated the first of the eight Coastal Surveillance Radar Systems (CARS) being set up by India in the country. Similarly India extended maritime security cover to Mozambique during the African Union Summit in 2003 and during the World Economic Forum at Maputo in 2004. In 2006 the two countries signed an MOU on defence cooperation that included among other things, joint patrolling off the Mozambican coast. More importantly, in a bid to check the surge in piracy off the Somali coast, the Indian navy has been undertaking constabulary duties in the Gulf of Aden since 2008, and has successfully escorted over 3000 vessels.[11] Multilaterally, India and Indian Ocean littoral countries within Africa are members of the Indian Ocean Rim Association of Regional Cooperation (IOARC) now renamed as the Indian Ocean Rim Association (IORA). Since assuming the chair in 2011, India has been working towards the revival of the institution and the expansion of its agenda to include security issues, apart from the economic issues. This was mainly driven by the growing security threats in the Indian Ocean region such as rise of piracy off Somali coast, increasing terror strikes by Al Qaeda affiliate Al Shabab in Somalia and neighbouring countries and to some extent China's forays in the Indian Ocean region.[12] The 2011, Bengaluru communiqué identified, six main areas of cooperation: Maritime Safety and Security; Trade and Investment Facilitation; Fisheries Management; Disaster Risk Reduction; Academic and S&T Cooperation; and Tourism Promotion and Cultural Exchanges.[13] India is also cooperating on security issues with South Africa and Brazil at the IBSA Dialogue forum.[14] The navies of the three countries have been involved in IBSAMAR naval exercises, which not only help in building mutual trust and interoperability but also underscore the strategic links between three important emerging powers in Indian Ocean and the South Atlantic region.

Way Forward

Apart from bilateral security issues, India and Africa share common concerns relating to global issues such as the menace of international terrorism, piracy, communicable diseases, energy insecurity, drug trafficking, climate change and environmental degradation, the challenge of providing food security to all, threats to cyber and space security and the long pending reform of United Nations Security Council. There are number of steps that can be taken to further strengthen the security engagement between India and Africa. First, in the global security context the security challenges have increasingly become multi-dimensional and are common to both India and the African countries. So there is a need for both to come together and devise common solutions to deal with these challenges. Second, as India's model of cooperation with Africa is based on prioritising African needs, India can match its initiatives in the continent with African initiatives such as the Agenda 2063 that sets out a vision for a peaceful, united and prosperous Africa. Third, on the issue of global governance reform both India and Africa support the greater democratisation of this institution. However both sides need to develop a greater understanding each other's positions to smoothen any differences that may emerge in the future. Fourth, India should scale up its intelligence and counter-terrorism linkages with African countries as well as at the continental level; and in the near term, forge a comprehensive counter-terror cooperation with the AU. Finally, In order to discuss, debate and develop a cooperative framework on security issues it is important for India and Africa to institutionalise a regular official dialogue on the side-lines of the India Africa Forum Summit.

NOTES

1. "African economic growth: The twilight of the resource curse? "*Economist* , January 10, 2015 at http://www.economist.com/news/middle-east-and-africa/21638141-africas-growth-being-powered-things-other-commodities-twilight (Accessed June 15, 2015)
2. 'India and United Nations peacekeeping and peace building' at https://www.pminewyork.org/pages.php?id= (Accessed May 30, 2015) See also 'Financing peacekeeping ' at http://www.un.org/en/peacekeeping/operations/financing.shtml (Accessed May 30, 2015)
3. 'UN peacekeeping operations in Africa: change in 2013 and Priorities for 2014' London, Chatham House, January 13, 2014 at http://www.chathamhouse.org/sites/default/files/home/chatham/public_html/sites/default/files/130114peacekeeping.pdf (Accessed September 30, 2015)
4. Saurabh Mishra and Keerthi Sampath Kumar, "India's Two Years at the Horse-Shoe Table", *IDSA Comment,* March 4, 2013 at http://www.idsa.in/issuebrief/IndiasTwoYearsattheHorseShoeTable_KeerthiSaurabh.html (Accessed March 10, 2014)
5. United Nations, Security Council, Record of the 7196th meeting on *United Nations Peace Keeping Missions: New Trends,* June 11, 2014
6. Ibid.
7. 'India pledges five million credit to Africa' at http://articles.economictimes.indiatimes.com/2011-05-25/news/29581729_1_india-pledges-african-nations-credit-line (Accessed September 30, 2014) *See also* 'India pledges $1 billion to UN backed mission in Mali' at http://economictimes.indiatimes.com/topic/African-led-International-Support-Mission-to-Mali (Accessed September 30, 2014)
8. PTI, "Hamid Ansari to represent India at the 50th African Union Summit", *Economic Times* May 24, 2013 http://articles.economictimes.indiatimes.com/2013-05-24/news/39501863_1_mea-official-external-affairs-ministry-african-union-summit (Accessed March 10 , 2014)
9. PTI, "India in position to be net provider of security: Manmohan Singh", *Live Mint,* May 23, 2013 at http://www.livemint.com/Politics/vlLjzXlM6ibZs1Zhd4OPFM/India-in-position-to-be-net-provider-of-security-in-region.html (Accessed September 28, 2015)
10. "India to develop strategic assets in 2 Mauritius, Seychelles islands" *Indian Express,* March

12, 2015 at: http://indianexpress.com/article/india/india-others/india-seychelles-sign-four-pacts-to-boost-security-cooperation/#sthash.qouaBIFb.dpuf (Accessed September 28, 2015)

11. "Good will visits by Indian naval ships to Oman" *Times of Oman*, October 6 2014 at http://www.timesofoman.com/article/41320/Oman/Goodwill-visit-by-Indian-Naval-ships-to-Oman (Accessed September 26, 2015)
12. C Raja Mohan, India's new role in the Indian Ocean. *Seminar*, 2011 at http://www.india-seminar.com/2011/617/617_c_raja_mohan.htm (Accessed September 5, 2014)
13. Ministry of External Affairs, Government of India, "Indian Ocean Rim Association for Regional Co-operation (IOR-ARC)", October 16, 2012 at http://mea.gov.in/in-focus-article.htm?20707/Indian+Ocean+Rim+Association+for+Regional+Cooperation+IORARC (Accessed March 12, 2014)
14. Daniel Flemes and Alcides Costa Vaz, *Security Policies of India, Brazil and South Africa: regional security contexts as constraints for a common agenda*, Mural Internacional, January–June, 2014 at http://www.e-ublicacoes.uerj.br/index.php/muralinternacional/article/viewFile/10863/9208 (Accessed December 14, 2014)

3

Countering Terrorism and Extremism in Africa: Drawing Lessons from the Indian Experience

Festus Kofi Aubyn

Introduction

Terrorism and extremism are the greatest security challenges facing the African continent. Although this is not a recent phenomenon, the growth of extremist groups, the rising numbers of attacks, sophistication and their transnational nature is becoming a matter of increasing concern for most countries on the continent. The African Union Annual Terrorism Situational Analysis and Statistical Report in 2013, for instance, recorded 755 terrorist attacks which resulted in 6902 terrorism related death of which, 2043 were terrorists.[1] A particularly worrisome trend is the alleged collusion between some extremist/terrorist groups such as the Al-Shabaab of Somalia and the Al-Qaeda in the Islamic Maghreb (AQIM) and the Al-Qaeda in South Asia. This paper, examines the threat of terrorism and extremism in Africa and some of the mechanisms initiated at the national and regional level to combat it. It begins by giving a succinct overview of terrorism and extremism in Africa focusing specifically on events in West,

North and East Africa. This is followed by an assessment of the possible implications of terrorism on regional and global security. The next section studies the steps taken by African states and regional organisations to combat terrorism/extremism. Most importantly, since terrorism is a global problem and cannot be effectively managed or resolved by any single country or entity, the paper explores the various ways in which India and Africa can work together to manage this imminent threat in the last section. Specifically, the paper underscores some of the useful lessons that can be learnt from India's experience in dealing with terrorism. Africa's cooperation with India in this respect is particularly imperative in view of the established links between the Al-Qaeda in South Asia and the Al-Shabaab and AQIM in Africa. These strategic links undoubtedly make India, which is both a victim of terrorism and a member of the South Asian Association for Regional Cooperation (SAARC), an important partner in the fight against this threat in Africa. The paper argues that terrorism is not just a military problem; it is also a social, economic, political, technological and ideological problem. For that reason, a viable counter-terrorism strategy should not only focus on using hard power but soft power as well. In other words, a multi-pronged approach that strikes a balance between the military approach, and a sustained effort to simultaneously address the causes of terrorism/extremism, which include specious ideologies, poor governance, human rights violations, poverty, corruption, marginalisation, social and economic injustice; as well as issues such as drug trafficking, maritime piracy, money laundering, and illegal arms trafficking, needs to be adopted.

Brief Overview of Terrorism and Extremism in West, North and East Africa

Africa is not new to the threats posed by terrorism and religious fundamentalism. During the struggle for independence and decolonisation, many of the activities of the freedom fighters were labelled as 'terrorist' activities.[2] However, since the terrorist attacks in Kenya and Tanzania in August 1998 and the subsequent 9/11 attacks in the United States, the issue has taken centre stage in both policy and academic discourse. Suffice it to say that, terrorism in Africa is no longer an imagined or emerging threat, as it was perceived to be a decade ago. It is now a real security challenge that does not only affect a particular region or country but the entire continent due in part to the all-pervasive poor governance, under-development, poverty, unemployment, and conflicts. The past few years, especially have seen a rise in the number of deadly attacks and the multiplicity of active terror networks with growing links to Al-Qaeda. While no region of the continent is particularly immune from the terrorist threat, the Sahel region of West Africa, Northern Nigeria, North Africa and East Africa, specifically the Horn of Africa, appear to be the hubs of regional and international terrorist attacks and activities.

In West Africa, especially the Sahel region, the most well-known and verifiable terrorist/extremist groups, whose operations threaten the stability of the region are: the Al-Qaeda in the Islamic Maghreb (AQIM); the Movement for Unity and Jihad in West Africa (MUJAO); Ansar Dine[3]; Ansaru; and Boko Haram.[4] These groups have grown in reach and sophistication and intensified their operations since the Libyan crisis, with their operations spreading across Mali, Algeria, Mauritania, Niger, Chad, Cameroon and Northern Nigeria. They are taking advantage of the structural weakness of these states, the porous borders and the socio-economic discontent of the population. Besides claiming responsibility for the many attacks on government buildings, security posts, schools and foreign diplomatic missions, these extremist groups especially, AQIM, and MUJAO have been responsible for several cases of kidnapping and the murders of Western tourists, aid and humanitarian workers, and security personnel in the Sahel region. In 2012, emboldened by the power vacuum in Mali, AQIM together with the MUJAO, and Ansar Dine, supported the National Movement for the Liberation of Azawad (MNLA) to take control of nearly two-thirds of Mali.[5] Until the intervention of the French Forces and the African-led International Support Mission in Mali (AFISMA), these rebel groups controlled the northern part of Mali and imposed a strict form of Sharia law on the local population.[6] On 3 November, 2013, two French journalists namely, Ghislaine Dupont and Claude Verlon were murdered outside Kidal, the birthplace of the MNLA, (the Tuareg separatist movement) by AQIM operatives. Boko Haram has also expanded its insurgency to neighbouring countries, including Cameroon, Chad and Niger. The group has been behind several bomb attacks on military and police installations, and has also claimed responsibility for similar attacks in the northern states of Nigeria such as Borno, Kaduna, Kano, Jos and border towns in Cameroon and Chad, killing thousands of people. In April 2014, Boko Haram kidnapped over 200 girls in Chibok in northern Nigeria, drawing global attention to the magnitude of their activities. A more worrying trend is that apart from the kidnappings and killings, the AQIM and its affiliates are working with cartels and other criminal networks in the region to smuggle drugs, arms, and other contraband goods to augment their resources and finances for continuing operations.[7] In 2009, three nationals were arrested and charged with 'plotting to transport cocaine across Africa with the intent to support al Qaeda, and its local affiliate AQIM and the Revolutionary Armed Forces of Colombia (FARC) in Ghana.[8]

In North Africa, the post Arab Spring has witnessed the resurgence and renewed momentum of Salafist-Jihadist movements due to the weakness of governments across the region. Libya represents the most active sanctuary for Salafi-jihadist groups in North Africa. Examples of these Salafi-jihadist groups include Ansar al-Sharia in Libya, Egypt, Tunisia and Mauritania, who are credited for sending fighters to Syria to strengthen the ranks of different Jihadists groups operating there.[9]

East Africa and the Horn of Africa on the other hand, form Africa's underbelly for global terrorism. Countries such as Somalia, Djibouti, Ethiopia, Kenya, Tanzania, Sudan, South Sudan and Uganda have, at various times, served as terrorist safe havens, staging areas, or transit points.[10] The region's porous borders, proximity to the Arabian Peninsula, weak law enforcement and judicial institutions, all-pervasive corruption, and, in some cases, state complicity in terrorist activities, combined with over two decades of instability in Somalia, have provided an enabling environment for Al-Qaeda and other violent extremist groups.[11] In the early 1990s, Sudan, for example, provided a safe haven for terrorists, including Osama bin Laden, before he was expelled in May 1996. It was also a gateway for various terrorist groups such as Al-Qaeda and Al Ittihad Al Islamiya[12] (AIAI, or Al Ittihad), to operate in the greater Horn of Africa.[13] In contemporary times, Harakat al-Shabaab al-Mujahideen (Al Shabaab), remains the main source of terrorist threat in the region, particularly in Somalia and Kenya. Al Shabaab employs extremist intimidation and terror tactics to instil fear in the population. It has been responsible for several kidnappings, shootings, and targeted political assassinations over the years. Among the well known terrorist attacks in East Africa are: the killing of 18 American soldiers in Mogadishu, Somalia in 1993; the 1998 bombing of American embassies in Nairobi, Kenya, and Dar es Salaam, Tanzania that killed over 200 people and injured more than 4,000; the car bombing of the Israeli-owned Paradise Hotel in Mombasa, Kenya on November 28, 2002; and the recent Westgate shopping mall attack by Al Shabaab, that claimed the lives of over 60 people in October 2013. Apart from Al Shabaab, groups such as the Lord Resistance Army (LRA) and the Allied Democratic Forces/National Army for the Liberation of Uganda (ADF/NALU) also poses serious security threats to states in the region especially, Uganda.

Implications of Terrorism and Extremism on Regional Security

There is no doubt that one of the greatest challenges to the stability of African states is terrorism/extremism. Already, most of the states that have fallen victims to terrorist attacks are grappling with its political, economic and social impacts. In particular, the increasingly rate of attacks has affected trade, businesses and investments, the aviation and tourism industry, and disrupted infrastructure. The possible security implications of the increasing terrorist and extremist attacks are numerous and diverse.

In West Africa and the Sahel region, despite the positive gains made by the French forces, the AFISMA and the UN forces in capturing most territories in Northern Mali after the 2012 political crises, some parts of the area like Kidal is still under the control of the rebel groups—the MNLA to be precise. In addition, vast areas of the Sahel region still lack an adequate state presence. Given the fragile nature of the security situation in the region, the threat posed by the expansion and increasing consolidation of groups such as AQIM and MUJAO is apparent. In fact, the Sahel region risks becoming a safe haven for jihadists, from all manner of backgrounds, and a springboard for further terrorist attacks outside the region. Secondly, there is an abundance of unemployed yet well-armed and military-trained men who could be recruited by the AQIM, MUJAO and Boko Haram, or could even turn to crime. What this means is that, regional vulnerabilities such as state fragility and porous borders in the Sahel, could promote criminal and terrorist activities. In other words, these groups will resort to kidnapping of tourists, foreign journalists and aid workers for huge ransoms[14] and engage in transnational organised crimes such as drug and arms trafficking, to grow their resource base and further develop their operational strength for sustained attacks.[15] Given that most acts of violence, conflicts and terrorist activities in the West African sub-region are fuelled by proceeds of drug trafficking and organised crime, the increased criminal activities will put at risk the very foundation of viable democratic states, and undermine governance, rule of law, human rights, socio-economic development, and stability in the region.[16] The recent instability in Guinea Bissau demonstrates the impact that unchecked organised criminal activity and trafficking could have in the region. A report by the *United Nations Office on Drugs and Crime* (*UNODC*) estimates that in 2008, the value of the cocaine transported through the country, was higher than the entire national income.[17] Lastly, the activities of Boko Haram have worrying implications for West African states with weak governance and state institutions. Now, its activities have been recorded in neighbouring countries like Niger and is likely to extend to other countries if not well checked. It is also important to note that any instability in Nigeria, which is the regional hegemon, may have serious security implications for the entire sub-region.

In East Africa, the activities of Al-Shabaab and its affiliates are affecting the stability of states in the region. The kidnapping and killing of foreign nationals and aid workers from Western countries are rife, as evident in the kidnapping of Georges Vandenbeusch, a French Priest in Koza, in Northern Cameroon near the Nigerian border.[18] Religious co-existence between Christians and Muslims especially, has also been affected as attacks on the former by Islamic extremist groups have triggered or elicited retributive attacks in countries like Kenya.[19] Al Shabaab in Somalia may also resort to transnational organised crime such as piracy to augment their financial base for further operations. This will affect maritime security in the Gulf of Aden.

Efforts to Combat Terrorism in Africa: National and Regional Level Initiatives

The fight against terrorism and extremism in Africa has been going on for decades. Counter-terrorism measures in Africa exist at four levels: national, sub-regional, continental and global. The focus of this paper, however, is on the national, regional and continental level initiative. At the national level, several anti-terrorism legislative frameworks have been put in place together with the establishment of counter-terrorist units. In East Africa, countries such as Tanzania, Uganda and Kenya have all passed anti-terrorism legislation in response to the threat. Kenya, for example, formed a special counter-terrorist unit in 2003 to deal with terrorism in the country. However, in West Africa, most of the country level counter-terrorism initiatives are in cooperation with other states and organisations such as the United States, and the European Union. The United States, for example, cooperates with countries such as Algeria, Tunisia, Morocco, Senegal, Ghana and Nigeria under the Trans-Sahara Counter Terrorism Initiative (TSCTI).[20] Apart from this, the US is also cooperating with countries in the Horn of Africa to combat terrorism through its East Africa Counter-Terrorism Initiative (EACTI) and the Combined Joint Task Force – Horn of Africa (CJTF-HOA). For the most part, these counter-terrorism initiatives have focused on detecting, disrupting and defeating transnational terrorist groups; countering the resurgence of international terrorism; and building the capacity of security agencies through training programmes.[21]

At the sub-regional level, response to terrorism and extremism remains fragile. In West Africa, the Authority of Heads of State and Government of the Economic Community of West African States (ECOWAS) in February 2013 adopted a Political Declaration on a Common Position against Terrorism, which included a Counter-Terrorism Strategy and Implementation Plan. Whether, this Declaration and Strategy can solve the complicated problem of terrorism in West Africa is yet to be seen as it is yet to be fully operational.[22] In East Africa and the Horn of Africa, the Intergovernmental Authority on Development (*IGAD*) in 2003 adopted an Implementation Plan to Counter Terrorism in the region. The plan focuses on the adoption of common legal frameworks, extradition, increased information exchange, training coordination, and international cooperation and highlights the importance of respecting human rights while countering terrorism. Other sub-regional groups are also in the process of developing counter terrorism strategies.[23] But in general terms, most of the regional counter-terrorism initiatives are in partnerships with the US and its G-8 allies, the Counter Terrorism Executive Directorate (CTED) of the United Nations Security Council, the UN Office on Drugs and Crime (UNODC), African Union, and the European Union.[24] These partnerships, provide technical and capacity-building assistance to states within the Regional Economic Communities (RECs).[25]

At the continental level, the Constitutive Act of the AU provides the basis for preventing and combating terrorism in Africa—Article 4(o) calls for "respect for the sanctity of human life, condemnation and rejection of impunity and political assassination, acts of terrorism and subversive activities."[26] Other AU documents that deal with acts of terrorism and extremism are the Peace and Security Council (PSC) protocol; the AU Non-Aggression and Common Defence Pact; and the Common African Defence and Security Policy (CADSP). However, efforts to combat terrorism and extremism date back to the era of the Organisation of African Unity (OAU). Early attempts at developing an African counter-terrorism regime began in June 1994 in Tunis, when African Leaders adopted the Declaration on a Code of Conduct for Inter-African Relations, at the 30th Ordinary Session of the Assembly.[27] This declaration among others, denounced extremism and terrorism particularly that which was based on political sectarianism, tribalism, ethnicity or religion, as undermining the moral and human values of peoples, particularly fundamental freedoms and tolerance. Following the terrorist attacks in Kenya and Tanzania in August 1998 and the need for a robust legislative framework to deal with the threat, led to the adoption of the OAU Convention on the Prevention and Combating of Terrorism (the Algiers Convention) at the 35th Ordinary Session of Heads of State and Government held in Algiers, Algeria, in July 1999.[28] This convention actually differentiated between acts of terrorism, and the acts committed by people in their struggle for self-determination. The convention also identified a number of terrorist offences and areas of cooperation among member states, apart from laying down guidelines for extradition. Because the convention failed to cover issues such as implementation mechanisms, human rights, terrorist financing, and the risk of terrorists acquiring weapons of mass destruction, a Protocol, to supplement the 1999 OAU Convention was adopted in 2004. A consequent Plan of Action on the Prevention and Combating of Terrorism led to the establishment, of an African Centre for the Study and Research on Terrorism (ACSRT) in Algiers.[29]

More significantly, in all these counter-terrorism initiatives, the challenge has not been the lack of frameworks and instruments to respond to the threat, but rather the excessive focus on the use of intelligence agencies, police and the judiciary. Though this is not bad in itself, it does not address the underlying causes or the issues that provide a fertile ground for terrorism and extremism to thrive. A comprehensive approach, focusing on governance, development, doctrinal issues and security has to be adopted at the regional and national levels in order to effectively deal with terrorism/extremism. This is where the lessons drawn from India's experience of dealing with terrorism and extremism are particularly imperative and instructive.

Lessons from the India's Experience in Dealing with Terrorism/Extremism

India has been a victim of terrorism, extremism and insurgency since its inception in 1947 in places such as Kashmir, Jammu and Punjab.[30] Some of these groups include the Pakistan based Lashkar-e-Tayyeba, Jaish-e-Mohammad, Harkat-ul-Mujahideen, Harkat-ul-Jihadi from Bangladesh, the Indian Mujahideen, and the Maoists.[31] In spite of the countless terrorist attacks and insurgencies, India has not allowed it to destabilise the country. It has managed the challenge relatively well, as a law and order problem. India has adopted a comprehensive approach that deals with terrorism as a phenomenon that has security, political, economic, social, psychological, operational and diplomatic aspects, all of which need equal attention.[32] The Indian counter-terrorism strategy has been to win the 'hearts and minds' of the people, so as to deny the terrorist moral and material support, with the minimum use of force.[33] This is perhaps one of the most important lesson Africa can learn from India. How a country as diverse as India been able to manage the threat of terrorism/extremism without collapsing, is something African countries can learn, and adapt in counter terrorism efforts on the continent. Indeed, these are useful lessons that India can share with African states in order to collectively deal with the threat. Apart from this, Africa and India can also cooperate to share intelligence on terrorist activities within both regions to counter terrorist plots, taking cognisance of the strategic links between terrorists groups in Africa and South Asia.

Conclusion

In conclusion, terrorism and extremism are global problems that affect every country in the world, directly or indirectly. India and Africa are both victims of terrorist and extremist attacks. The two regions can work together at the multilateral level to fight the external dimensions of terrorism and extremism in their respective regions, since an effective counter-terrorism strategy should have political, legal, military, technological, social and economic dimensions.

NOTES

1. African Union, *Annual Terrorism Situational Analysis and Statistical Report,* African Centre for the Study and Research on Terrorism, Algiers, 2013.
2. Martin Ewi and Kwesi Aning, "Assessing the Role of the African Union in Preventing and Combating Terrorism in Africa," *African Security Review,* 15(3), 2006; Cyril Obi, "Terrorism in West Africa: Real, Emerging Or Imagined Threats?" *African Security Review* 15(3), p.89, 2006.
3. Ansar Dine has disappeared since the French and AFISMA intervention in Mali in January 2013.
4. See Kwesi Aning and Festus Aubyn, "Confronting the threats of Boko Haram Crises in Northern Nigeria: Exploring Options for a Peaceful Settlement," *Stability Operations,* Vol. 8, No. 1, 2012.
5. Kwesi Aning and Festus Aubyn, "Challenges in Mali: Historic duty to ensure peace," *New Routes,* No. 2, 2013.
6. Ibid.
7. Modibo Goita, "West Africa Growing Terrorist Threat: Confronting AQIM's Sahelian Strategy "*Africa Security Brief,* No.11, 2011.
8. Kwesi Aning, *Organised Crime in West Africa: Options for EU Engagement,* International IDEA, Vienna, UNODC, 2009.
9. African Union, n.1.
10. Peter Kagwanja, "Counter-Terrorism in the Horn of Africa: New Security Frontiers, Old Strategies," *Africa Security Review,* Vol. 15, No. 3, 2006.
11. Lauren Ploch, 'Countering Terrorism in East Africa: The U.S. Response' *CRS Report for Congress, 2010.*
12. The AIAI was defeated by the Ethiopian military in a series of battles in 1996 and 1997.
13. Ibid.

14. AQIM has fetched ransoms as high as $6 million in one instance and accumulated tens of millions of dollars in kidnapping fees since 2006. Charlie Warren, "Terrorism in West Africa: The Anarchy That Hasn't Come" http://africanarguments.org/2012/05/30/terrorism-in-west-africa-the-anarchy-that-hasn't-come-by-charlie-warren/ (Accessed on May 30, 2012).
15. Kwesi Aning, *Organized Crime in West Africa: Options for EU Engagement International* IDEA publication; Stockholm, 2009, *Transnational Trafficking and the Rule of Law in West Africa: A Threat Assessment,* Vienna, UNODC, 2009.
16. Ibid.
17. See "Threats to Peace and Security in West Africa and the Sahel Region" http://www.securitycouncilreport.org. Accessed January 10, 2013.
18. See "French priest kidnapped in Cameroon" http://www.bbc.co.uk/news/world-africa-24936965 (Accessed November 13, 2013).
19. "Ripple Effects of a Terrorist Attack: After Westgate, Kenya and the World Face Changing Times" *International Business Times,* http://www.ibtimes.com/ripple-effects-terrorist-attack-after-westgate-kenya-world-face-changing-times-1409654. Accessed November 10, 2013.
20. Kwesi Aning and Festus Aubyn, "Negotiating the pitfalls of peace and security in Africa and a New American Grand Strategy: APSA and AFRICOM" in Volker C. Franke and Robert H. Dorff (eds.), *Conflict Management and Peacebuilding: Pillars of a New American Grand Strategy,* Strategic Studies Institute of the US Army War College, Washington, 2013.
21. Ibid.
22. Martin Ewi, "The new ECOWAS Counter-Terrorism Strategy and its implications for West Africa". http://www.issafrica.org/iss-today/the-new-ecowas-counter-terrorism-strategy-and-its-implications-for-west-africa. Accessed February 24, 2015.
23. "Fighting Terror through Justice: Implementing the IGAD Framework for Legal Cooperation against Terrorism" *Final Report of the Task Force on Legal Cooperation against Terrorism in the IGAD Sub region,* Centreon Global Counterterrorism Cooperation, 2013.
24. Cyril. Obi, "Terrorism in West Africa: Real, emerging or imagined threats?" *African Security Review,* 15(3), 2006; K.A. Bolaji, "Preventing Terrorism in West Africa: Good Governance or Collective Security?" *Journal of Sustainable Development in Africa,* 12(1), 2010.
25. Ibid.
26. See the AU Constitutive Act, 2002.
27. For more information on this see Martin Ewi and Kwesi Aning, "Assessing the Role of the African Union in Preventing and Combating Terrorism in Africa," *African Security Review,* 15(3), 2006.
28. Ibid.
29. For more information see http://www.caert.org.dz/an/reports.php. Accessed on November 5, 2013.
30. Anand Kumar (ed), *The Terror Challenge in South Asia and Prospect of Regional Cooperation,* IDSA, New Delhi, 2012.
31. It is instructive to note that most of these groups have links with Al Qaeda and also have global ambitions.
32. Arvind Gupta, Ashok Behuria, P.V. Ramana and Pushpita Das, "India's Experience in Dealing with Terrorism" in Anand Kumar (ed.), *The Terror Challenge in South Asia and Prospect of Regional Cooperation,* IDSA, New Delhi, 2012.
33. Ibid.

4

Rise of Terrorism/Extremism in India: Lessons for Africa

Vivek Chadha

India has been grappling with terrorism/extremism for over five decades. During this period, the country has faced indigenous threats, as well as an externally sponsored proxy war. This has given the country the unique experience of fighting terrorism. India's experience of dealing with terrorism/extremism has provided useful insights and has been for long a subject for research. The counter terrorism skills developed at various levels have also been shared with a number of friendly countries in the past. This not only includes valuable lessons learnt from the successes, but also the failures. Past experience indicates that failures not only highlight systemic weaknesses, they are also critical catalysts for inducing change.

A brief over view of the worldwide evolution of terrorism highlights the different stages in the progression of this threat. The late 19th century saw the rise of anarchism, which abhorred the very idea of government.[1] As a result, a series of high visibility assassinations were witnessed in countries like Russia and France. The freedom movements against colonial powers in the mid-20th century prompted the next major wave of terrorism.[2] The examples of Algeria, Kenya, Palestine, are amongst the few where there was violence during this period. The third wave was spearheaded by communist revolutionary movements in the Cold War years. Groups and countries received the support of communist regimes and a wave of violence followed. The end of the Cold War and the disintegration of Soviet Union, brought this chapter of terrorism to an end. The fourth generation of terrorism emerged from the shadow of religious fundamentalism and extremism. It propagated violence on the basis of religion and claimed sanction for violent actions in the name of God. The Al Qaeda is the most prominent example, of this and the 9/11 attack became its calling card.

This broad classification not only provides an overview of terrorism's progression over the years but also its diverse motivations. However, the Indian example and possibly a number of other cases in Africa suggest that these classifications are neither sacrosanct nor rigid. Each case of terrorism, in a particular part of the world, has its own distinct character and roots. Therefore, such generic classifications are accompanied by inherent contradictions. India, even after six decades of independence, continues to struggle with a wide range of insurgencies, terrorism and extremism, which fall into different categories. This reinforces the need to assess each group and region in its specific context, to arrive at a solution, which has local roots and a global appeal.

Threat of Terrorism/Extremism in India

Purely from a geographical point of view, the internal security (IS) challenges faced by India can be located in four distinct areas. The oldest insurgencies continue to simmer in the Northeastern region of the country. The Naga insurgents took up arms in 1955, and despite a series of half settlements, and a ceasefire, a final peace settlement remains elusive.[3] Mizoram is yet another state, which saw a section of its population take up arms in 1966. However, unlike the Naga insurgency, the Mizo National Front (MNF) chose to negotiate a settlement in 1986.[4] In a unique display of political maturity, the leader of the MNF, Laldenga, became the first chief minister of the newly created state. Both these insurgencies were marked by classical guerrilla warfare, similar to that witnessed during the various phases of communist revolutionary struggles. A number of other uprisings have taken place in this region, each with its distinct characteristics.

India also faces terrorism in the northern state of Jammu and Kashmir (J&K). What started as an indigenous movement in a small part of the state, was hijacked by Pakistan, in an attempt to carry forward its agenda of wresting the state from India. The struggle in J&K was given a distinct religious overtone in a bid to artificially give it a homogenous character and link it with Pakistan. This effort can best be described as contrived, since the state has for ages had a moderate, secular and tolerant society. This ethos, better known as *Kashmiriyat*, characterises Kashmiri society, enriched over centuries by moderate Sufi traditions.[5] Today J&K faces violence because of terrorism which is spawned in an environment of extremism in Pakistan, nurtured to perpetuate violence in the name of *jehad*, funded by donations and illegal sources of money and directed by state intelligence agencies.[6]

The third region, is also the largest in terms of the geographical spread, and hugs the eastern coast of the country. Spread over a number of states, the uprising is fuelled by Maoist thought and has been in the making for decades. However, it assumed threatening proportions in 2004, with the emergence of the CPI (Maoist).[7] The group remains determined to overthrow the existing democratically elected government through a people's revolution. It impacts almost a third of the country in terms of area and has resulted in more casualties than all the other regions put together.[8]

The fourth threat emerges from pan India terrorist groups like the Indian Mujahideen.[9] The group has been involved in a number of terrorist attacks across the country. It draws its support from fringe elements who believe that their community is being selectively prosecuted. They have undertaken a number of IED attacks, leading to the killing of a large number of innocents.[10] The group has been receiving support, training and guidance from Pakistan. Its modules in different parts of the country have an elusive hierarchy. The decentralised functioning of the group facilitates operational independence. This also makes it difficult to trace the inter-linkage of modules, thereby improving their chances of survival.

This brief overview clearly highlights the diverse threats faced by the country. It also reveals the motivations of some of these groups. The reality of the threats in the case of India will find resonance in Africa as well, where religious extremism, external support, ethnic divisions, secessionist demands and competition for resources are fuelling internal conflict.

Facets of the Indian Response

The threat of terrorism/extremism in India has witnessed an evolving response over the last six decades. This response can best be understood in terms of the various levels, at which it is planned and thereafter executed.

The fundamental guidance for tackling internal security challenges is provided by the highest political authority in the country. The political approach, from the period immediately following India's independence has been guided by the policy of accommodation of diverse opinions and negotiations with groups willing to negotiate peace within the framework of the Indian Constitution. Guerrilla fighters and their mentors have been regarded as misguided citizens of the country; and uprisings have been seen as violent expressions of political differences, that can be overcome through mutual conciliation. The first prime minister of the country, Pandit Jawaharlal Nehru, articulating this sentiment has been quoted as having said:

> But the military approach, while necessary, was not adequate; and Nehru insisted that soldiers and officials should always remember that the Nagas were fellow-countrymen, who were not merely to be suppressed but, at some stage had to be won over.[11]

This sentiment was echoed by the chief of army staff, prior to the induction of the army for counter insurgency (CI) operations highlighted the need to fight terrorism, even as the people are protected from violence.

> You are not there to fight the people in the area, but to protect them. You are fighting only those who threaten the people and who are a danger to the lives and properties of the people.[12]

This political flexibility has been evident in the past, whereby: negotiations have led to creation of new states within the country; grant of socio-economic autonomy to districts within existing states; recognition and support for languages in order to maintain the distinct identity of ethnic groups; and amendments to the Constitution of India to give special status to states like J&K.[13] This political flexibility is possibly one of the major reasons that has enabled a country as diverse as India to remain united and give a sense of identity to different sections of the society. This therefore, is possibly the most important lesson gleaned from India's experience with extremist groups and ideas.

Second, this political approach is accompanied by a dual track policy of security and development. Several areas, where terrorism and extremism have taken root, have been relatively under developed. This prompted the government to undertake wide ranging developmental initiatives, along with simultaneous efforts to ensure the security of the people and the neutralisation of terrorist violence. This approach is tweaked by regulating the inter-se emphasis on these two aspects. To illustrate, there is a greater emphasis on security in an area which has a very high level security threat, and conversely, as the security situation improves, developmental work is given a fillip. This approach also reinforces the need for equitable growth, the absence of which in some regions of India in the past, provided extremists with the ideal conditions to nurture insurgency. This remains an important lesson for all developing countries, in the midst of rapid economic transition in their societies.

Third, India has a three tiered security response mechanism to deal with internal threats. This consists of: the local police in the initial stages, central police forces at the next stage and finally the armed forces. While there is an attempt to deal with such threats at the first two levels, but in a number of cases, especially from the mid-fifties, the armed forces have been involved in CI operations. This is not an ideal situation, however, it does provide for a fall back option of early induction of the armed forces, if they are trained for such contingencies. India's experience has shown that there have been apparent weaknesses in the training of security forces in general, and the state and central police forces in particular, specifically with reference to counter terrorism and extremism. This is further accentuated by the fact that since law and order is a state subject as per the country's constitution, there is a wide variation in the standard of policing across states. Weaknesses of policing in some states have crept in because of inadequate investment in raising the requisite numbers and the building up of the necessary capacities of state police forces. Former home minister, P. Chidambaram highlighted the acute shortage of police in the country. As of January 1, 2008, this figure was less than 50 per cent of the international average of 270 policemen per a lakh of population.[14]

There is a direct co-relation between the capacity of police forces in states and the emergence of terrorism and extremism. In more cases than not, state police forces have not been successful in curbing violence in the incubatory stages, leading to the induction of central police. Given the wide variety of roles undertaken by central police units, from election duties to disaster relief, their capability to counter terrorism as specialist forces been affected adversely. A former army chief highlighted the problem, when he said, "There are certain problem areas in training. At times we don't get a homogenous entity for training. This means the entire company does not come for training."[15] More often than not, this has led to the induction of army into CI operations, which rather than being the instrument of last resort, has become the most first choice in times of crisis.

These three tiers have also been employed simultaneously in some areas of operations. As an example, the state of J&K, witnessed deployment of the army on the Line of Control (LoC), the Rashtriya Rifles, a para military force in the hinterland and the central and state police forces in urban areas. This created a system of a tiered state response, wherein, the process of reestablishment of governance through the local police force, simultaneously accompanies the blocking of external threats on the LoC by the army.

The fourth critical characteristic of the Indian response has been the time factor. In most cases, a protracted conflict by weaker extremists is seen as a tool to steadily chip away at the power of a stronger state. This provides the extremists with an opportunity to build up their resources and capability to a level, which will enable them to overwhelm the state. This is related to the lack of popular support for the state, the weakening of state structures and increased external support for the uprising. This cycle has been visible in a number of civil wars and revolutions. Robert Taber in his book, *The War of the Flea* writes:

> Analogically, the guerrilla fights the war of the flea, and his military enemy suffers the dog's disadvantages: too much to defend; too small,

> ubiquitous, and agile an enemy to come to grips with. If the war continues long enough—this is the theory—the dog succumbs to exhaustion and anemia without ever having found anything on which to close his jaws or to rake with his claws.[16]

However, in the case of India, the state has successfully been able to reverse this trend. Terrorist and extremist groups have not been able to break the will of the state, despite decades of resistance. This can be seen in a comparative assessment of the average duration of insurgencies worldwide, with those in India. Amongst the 12 insurgencies analysed in case of India, the duration of the six resolved by the state, ranged from seven to 26 years, with an average of 16 years. However, in the case of the six, that remain unresolved, the average duration is 36 years. In comparison, the average duration of insurgencies worldwide has been 10 years.[17] It is evident from these figures that the Indian state has been more resilient to terrorism and extremism, which is a reflection of the core strength of the country. It is also a commentary on the nature of the challenge posed by such conflicts and possibly the psychological preparation necessary for state agencies and the people affected by it.

Fifth, the military response of security agencies has been characterised by restraint and a consistent desire to minimise collateral damage. This response has evolved as part of the Indian experience in the past, which did involve the employment of air power in an offensive role in Mizoram. However, experience has reinforced the futility of such a response because of the scope of collateral damage and its impact on innocent citizens. This thought process is not limited to air power alone, but extends to the employment of weapons like artillery, mortars and heavy machine guns. This approach is at a variance with some of the recent examples, which have come to light during the Iraq and Afghanistan campaigns led by the US. In contrast, Defence Minister A.K. Antony, ruled out the employment air power for offensive operations in Naxal areas, citing the likely collateral damage.[18] The aspect is reinforced by the army's doctrine for sub conventional operations, which states:

> The use of force should be judicious and governed by explicit rules of engagement that must hinge on the principle of "minimum force", besides taking into account the political, legal and moral stipulations.[19]

The *Doctrine for Sub Conventional Operations*, also clearly indicates the need for a nuanced approach, while dealing with extremists. This is geared to the different types of adversaries faced by the country. On the one hand, they include estranged citizens of the country, who have in the past taken up arms against the state. The state's attempts to facilitate their return into the national mainstream have been reasonably successful. On the other hand terrorists employed by Pakistan as part of a proxy war, aim to destabilise the country and kill innocent people. Their neutralisation thus becomes the principal aim of military operations.

Sixth, external factors plays an important role in India's counter terrorism policy. The threat ranges from direct support in the case of Pakistan, to the inability of countries like Myanmar, to influence and control their periphery, which is exploited as a safe sanctuary by terrorist groups. The Indian response mechanisms have been tailored in keeping with these threats.

Pakistan employs terrorists as part of its proxy war against India, and this is addressed at various levels. While there has been an endeavour to expose this linkage at international forums and during bilateral interactions, attempts have also been made to convince Pakistan regarding the futility and self-defeating consequences of such misadventures. Militarily, the army has been reasonably successful in limiting the infiltration of terrorists from across the LoC. The RR and police have further ensured that the ability of terrorists to shape the security environment in the state is minimised. This multi-pronged strategy remains a work in progress, but its relative success is evident from the decrease in the number of violent incidents over a period of time.[20]

Conclusion

The Indian experience clearly includes both successes and failures, in its fight against terrorism/extremism. It is evident that tackling terrorism is becoming increasing challenging, given the transnational character of threats, continued state sponsorship and sophistication of terror networks. Past experience indicates that it is easier to provide good governance and equitable growth, rather than having to undo the socio-economic isolation of segments of society while simultaneously dealing with violence. It is also important to calibrate the military response to minimise collateral damage and loss of popular support.

India as a developing country, faces challenges similar to those confronting Africa. Not only are some of the threats faced by the two countries similar, but the successful resolution thereof, can also become the basis for lessons. Amongst these, the experience gained in fighting terrorism remains one example. India's military experience can become a useful contributing tool for capacity building in Africa. Equally important is the process of institution building, which is essential, for the best utilisation of both military and civilian capabilities. This paper highlights some of the important lessons learnt by India, which can undoubtedly be used by affected countries in Africa, to better deal with the challenges of terrorism.

NOTES

1. For a detailed analysis of the four waves of terrorism see David C. Rapoport, *The Four Waves of Modern Terrorism*, http://www.international.ucla.edu/cms/files/Rapoport-Four-Waves-of-Modern-Terrorism.pdf (Accessed on November 16, 2013).
2. Brenda J. Lutz and James M. Lutz, *Global Terrorism*, New York, Routledge, 2008, p 103.
3. For an assessment of insurgencies in Northeast India see, B.G. Verghese, *India's Northeast Resurgent*, Delhi, Konark Publishers, 1991.
4. For the text of the Mizo Accord, 1986 see, http://www.satp.org/satporgtp/countries/india/states/mizoram/documents/papers/mizoram_accord_1986.htm, (Accessed on November 16, 2013).
5. See Vijay K Sazawal, "The True Meaning of Kashmiriyat", *Kashmir Forum*, February 6, 2009, http://www.kashmirforum.org/The%20True%20Meaning%20of%20Kashmiriyat.html, Accessed on November 16, 2013, for an understanding of Kashmiriyat.
6. "Infiltration attempts cannot take place without Pakistan Army support: Antony", *Deccan Chronicle*, October 30, 2013, http://www.deccanchronicle.com/131030/news-current-affairs/article/infiltration-attempts-cannot-take-place-without-pakistan-army, (Accessed on November 16, 2013).
7. See *Bannedthought.Net* for CPI (Maoist) documents giving a glimpse into their ideology, http://www.bannedthought.net/India/, Accessed on November 16, 2013.
8. *Annual Report 2012-13*, Ministry of Home Affairs, Government of India, pp. 6-18.
9. See Shishir Gupta, *Tracking the Indian Mujahideen: Tracking the Enemy Within*, Gurgaon, Hachette India, 2011 for the recent activities of the Indian Mujahideen.
10. *See Annual Report 2012-13*, Ministry of Home Affairs, n. 8, p. 18.
11. Sarvepalli Gopal, *Jawaharlal Nehru: A Biography, Vol. 2, 1947-1956*, Delhi, Oxford University Press, 1980.
12. Quoted in Rajesh Rajagopalan, *Fighting Like a Guerrilla: The Indian Army and Counterinsurgency*, New Delhi, Routledge, 2008, p. 147.
13. For the text of Article 370 see, http://lawmin.nic.in/coi/PARTXXI.pdf (Accessed on November 16, 2013).

14. P Chidambaram, "Home minister proposes radical restructuring of security architecture" December 23, 2009, http://pib.nic.in/newsite/erelease.aspx?relid=56395, Accessed on December 10, 2012.
15. "Army chief says CRPF training needs upgrade: willing to help", *The Indian Express*, April 09, 2010, http://www.indianexpress.com/news/army-chief-says-crpf-training-needs-upgrade-willing-to-help/602146/, (Accessed on, November 14, 2013)
16. Faber, Robert, *The War of the Flea: The Classic Study of Guerrilla Warfare*, Washington D.C., Potomac Books, 2002, p. 29.
17. Ben Connable and Martin C. Libicki, *How Insurgencies End*, Santa Monica RAND, 2010, p. 27.
18. Rajat Pandit, "No proposal to deploy army in Naxalite-hit areas: Antony", *Times of India*, May 28, 2013, http://articles.timesofindia.indiatimes.com/2013-05-28/india/39578593_1_counter-insurgency-armed-forces-ongoing-anti-naxal-operations, (Accessed on, November 14, 2013).
19. *Doctrine for Sub Conventional Operations*, Integrated Headquarters of Ministry of Defence (Army), Headquarters Army Training Command, Shimla, December 2006, p. 29.
20. *Annual Report 2012-13*, Ministry of Home Affairs, Government of India, pp. 6-7.

5

Terrorism in Africa: Implications for India

Manish Chand

The paper is divided into three parts. The first section maps out the spread of terrorism in Africa and the key terrorist and militant groups involved in it. It also examines a host of socio-economic reasons responsible for the spurt of terrorism in Africa; and the efforts made by African countries to counter the scourge. The second section studies the ramifications of the spread of terrorism in Africa for global security, and what it means for countries like India, which are scaling up their diplomatic, economic and energy ties with the African continent. The third section outlines the huge stakes India has in curbing terrorism in Africa and presents suggestions and recommendations for deepening security and counter-terror cooperation between India and the African continent.

Two Narratives

Over the last decade or so, a new narrative of Africa has emerged, which projects the continent as a growth pole of the world and a repository of opportunity. From the 'Hopeless Continent,' as Africa was despairingly dismissed by *The Economist* more than a decade ago, Africa is now widely seen as the 'Continent of Hope.' Ironically, it is the same influential British publication, among others, that is at the forefront of heralding an African renaissance. This narrative of Afro-optimism, which is also shared by India and other emerging economies who have perceptibly scaled up their engagement with the continent over the last decade, has subtly but incrementally, supplanted the narrative of conflict, catastrophe and chaos, which were used mindlessly to describe the continent, not so long ago. This new narrative of Africa as the hub of renaissance, resurgence and renewal, is, however, again in danger of being replaced with that of the three Cs—conflict, catastrophe and chaos—due to a host of security challenges. The rise of the spectre of terrorism in Africa, if not checked by the concerted efforts of the continent and its partners, could easily reverse the narrative of Afro-optimism to Afro-pessimism.

Terrorism in Africa

The rise of terrorism in Africa poses major threats not just for Africa, but for the increasingly connected world, both in economic and security terms. A joint communiqué issued by the Committee of Intelligence and Security Services of Africa in October, 2013 stated that the biggest threats to Africa's stability and security were terrorism and extremism. The meeting brought together more than a dozen intelligence chiefs of intelligence agencies from various African countries to discuss the escalating threat of terrorism and extremism in Africa and map out a joint strategy to scale up the intelligence infrastructure and coordination to deal with this growing menace.

The ramifications of the rise of terrorism for Africa's long-standing traditional partners as well as emerging countries like India, and the BRICS formation require a more focused analysis and the formulation of a multi-pronged strategy to deal with this many-headed threat, which is increasingly acquiring trans-national dimensions. The September 11, 2013 attack on the Westgate mall in Nairobi was a rude wake-up call for Africa, as well as the international community, to get their act together to individually and collectively deal with this scourge. Complacency is hardly an option; it's Nairobi today, and tomorrow it could be New York, New Delhi or Mumbai, and one should not be really surprised if future terror attacks in world capitals are traced back to the insidious terror networks operating in Sub-Saharan Africa or the Sahel region.

Types of Terrorism

Against this backdrop, it's important to appraise afresh the causes and the complex interplay of motivations that are fuelling the rise of terrorism and extremism in Africa. To begin with, it's important to underscore the multi-dimensionality of terrorism afflicting the African continent. Terrorism in Africa is not monolithic and homogenous, but is a hybrid many-headed creature.

For the purpose of analysis, terrorism in Africa can be classified into four broad genres or categories:

I) Ideology-based terrorism and extremism based on the appeal to radical Wahhabi Islam

II) Economics-based terrorism, which is rooted in a sense of alienation, deprivation and structural issues like underdevelopment, poverty and lack of adequate economic opportunities

III) Mercenary terrorism, which is basically used by terror entrepreneurs who exploit the sense of popular discontent and grievance to construct profitable business enterprises by blending narcotics, smuggling, kidnappings and arms-trade.

IV) Political terrorism, which is used by some groups like the Nigeria-based Boko Haram, to challenge the ruling dispensation and present themselves as a potential alternative or ruler.

Most leading terrorist groups in Africa like Al-Shabaab, which claimed responsibility for the Westgate mall terror, the Al-Qaeda in the Maghreb (AQIM) and Boko Haram are a blend of the four categories described above, and not exclusively, one or the other. According to Princeton N. Lyman, a former US ambassador to Nigeria and South Africa, besides these top three terror outfits there are a host of,

> organised rebellions or insurgencies in Africa, while not always classified as terrorists, which wreak terrible havoc on African people and threaten national stability. These include various militia in eastern Congo, who have been the target of the International Criminal Court for their crimes against humanity, the insurgents in the Niger delta of Nigeria, and the Janjaweed militia in the Darfur region of Sudan. It is notable that the U.S. African Command lists the Lord's Resistance Army, the Army for

> Liberation of Rwanda, and the obscure Afrikaner Boeremag in South Africa along with a host of Islamic groups as among the "Terror Groups in Africa."[1]

What is most frightening about all these terror groups, regardless of their near-term goals and objectives, is the use of radical Islam as a binding ideology, which makes them part of the global jihadi network. For example, Al-Shabaab, which is primarily confined to Somalia, emerged in response to widespread poverty, deprivation and underdevelopment in the Horn of Africa country. The militant group has increasingly used Wahhabism to rally the disaffected youth (Al-Shabaab means the "youth" in Arabic) and lure them with the seductive vision of a purist Islamist society. Its leader Ahmed Abdi Godane formally established ties with Al-Qaeda in 2012, and drums up support by using the language of international jihad. Thus, a group which started off as a local insurgency, is now trying to forge a more ambitious international jihad agenda. This was clear from its choice of the Westgate mall, the hub of expatriates of multiple nationalities, as a terror target.

According to Emily Mellgard, a Research Associate at the Africa programme of the Council on Foreign Relations (CFR), Al-Shabaab's activities can have an international impact.[2] Their attacks across international borders, like the attack on the Westgate mall in Nairobi, impact the international expatriate and tourist presence as well as international business interests, in addition to the devastation it wreaks on local communities and businesses. The Westgate mall is jointly owned by Kenyan and Israeli interests.

The evolution of Al-Qaeda in the Islamic Maghreb (AQIM) is another case study of the cynical use of radical Islam. The AQIM, which is active across much of the Sahel, is a hybrid amalgam of all the above-mentioned four categories of terrorism. On the one hand, the AQIM uses the kidnappings of foreigners, smuggling and arms trade to fund its operations (mercenary terrorism), while on the other hand the group's leaders conjure up an alluring picture of an Islamist paradise and invoke ancient Islamic empires that once thrived in the region. The AQIM espouses the stringent enforcement of Sharia law and also deploys virulently anti-Western rhetoric as a rallying tactic and has links with al-Qaeda.

The Nigeria-based Boko Haram started off as a localised radical insurgency and is primarily active across northern Nigeria, but its operatives are found to be crossing the porous borders into Niger, Cameroon, and even into Mali. Boko Haram also uses Wahabbi Islam as its ideological inspiration and "rejects as evil the secular federal government in Nigeria, seeks its destruction, and the establishment of an Islamic state in its place."[3] Emily Mellgard says that many of the radical teachers who proselytise Islamic radicalism in Nigeria are influenced by Islamic teachers based in Khartoum.[4] According to John Campbell, a former US ambassador to Nigeria, Boko Haram is "looking toward the creation of God's kingdom on earth through violence against those they see as Islam's enemies, rather than the achievement of a political programme."[5] In an hour-long video released on August 24, Boko Haram's emir, Abubakar Shekau, declared his intention to establish the world's second Islamic "caliphate."[6]

The emergence of Africa as a haven for terrorists is, therefore, driven by a host of tangled motivations. In an article in *The Atlantic* magazine, Yochi Dreazen lists some of the reasons that make the continent a hospitable territory for groups like AQIM and al-Shabaab.

Fears about Africa's emergence as a terror haven are unlikely to subside anytime soon. Africa's Islamists are able to take advantage of the fact that many of the continent's countries have porous borders; weak and corrupt central governments; undertrained and underequipped militaries; flourishing drug trades that provide a steady source of income; and vast, lawless spaces that are so large—and so far away from major American military bases like those in the Middle East and Afghanistan—that it would be difficult for the US to mount effective counter-terror efforts even if the war-weary Obama administration chose to do so. Those are precisely the reasons (along with a trove of Libyan weapons) Islamists were able to conquer northern Mali and use it as a base for planning the strikes on the uranium mine in Niger and the natural-gas plant in Algeria. Those are also the reasons American officials worry that a successful terror attack in the US or Europe planned in Africa and carried out by African extremists is only a matter of time. The new face of militant Islam, in other words, is likely to be an African one.[7]

Terrorism in Africa: Implications for India

Terrorism in Africa is marked by the emergence of the narrative of the other as the enemy. The other, in the imagination of radical Islamists, is the West and its perceived allies, the Enemy. In the radical Islamist or jihadi's imagination, India, despite its avowedly independent foreign policy, is increasingly seen as being in the Western camp, and hence could be a potential target.

The terror attack inside the swanky Westgate mall in Nairobi—the hostage-taking, the choice of the target and people of multiple nationalities who were victims—was all eerily reminiscent of the 26/11 Mumbai terror mayhem in November 2008, when ten Pakistan-based terrorists attacked the iconic Taj Mahal Hotel and also chose the Jewish Chabad House as one of their targets. Much like Mumbai in which more than 26 foreign nationals were killed, the casualties of the Nairobi bombings included, among others, two Indians, two Canadians, two French citizens, a South Korean, a South African, and a Dutch woman. The selection of the target—the Westgate shopping mall, which is partly owned by an Israeli company—underlined the hideous ideology of al-Qaeda-backed Somali terror group al-Shabaab, which owned responsibility for the attack. If anything, this underlined the ambitious ideological message behind the attack. In both cases, the larger target was the cosmopolitan culture of big cities and the ethos of liberalism. The message was aimed at the West and its allies to warn them from undertaking what militant Islamist ideologues, term anti-Islamic activities. In short, the immediate physical target was a mall in Nairobi, but the target audience was international as the news of the terror attack rippled across trans-national TV and media networks across the globe.

In the last decade, trans-national terror syndicates have attacked a host of cities—the terrorists' targets have invariably been big cities, with their inclusive ethos of absorbing diverse peoples and cultures. The fact that a world-class swanky shopping mall, which symbolises the aspirational African middle class and is thronged by affluent expatriates, including many Indians, was targeted provides some clues to the twisted ideology of the terrorists.

The Way Ahead

India, which has suffered multiple terror strikes over the years in the name of delusional and warped ideologies, has, therefore, many solid reasons to be concerned about the rising spiral of terrorism in Africa as it impacts its core national security interests and its growing engagement with the African continent, which pivots around trade, technology transfer and training. India's diplomatic energy is currently focused on the post-2014 Afghanistan transition process as international combat troops leave Afghanistan, making the country more vulnerable to assorted jihadi terror networks operating from Afghanistan. In this context, intelligence reports about the incestuous connections between some of militant groups active in West Africa and the Sahel region and Afghanistan are alarming.

Not many Indians can place Mali on the map right now, but it's possible that a potential terror attack in Mumbai and Delhi is plotted in the wastelands of Mali via Afghanistan. It's also instructive to remember that Osama bin Laden was mentored by Hassan Turabi in Sudan. In an interview with this writer in 2007 in Khartoum, Turabi had spoken about how some African jihadis from Sudan travelled to Kashmir in the 1990s as part of their global jihad mission. The situation can repeat itself if the Indian intelligence and security establishment is not fully seized of the trans-national connections of terror groups active in the continent.

It's time, therefore, for India to scale up its security and counter-terror cooperation with African countries individually, and on the continental level with the AU and its Peace and Security Council. The long-term solution to Africa's terrorism problem lies in addressing larger structural issues of poverty, underdevelopment, the widening rich-poor gap and misgovernance—weak and failing states provide a perfect haven for terrorists and extremists. India's policy-makers, therefore, need to make a conscious strategic decision to scale up its development partnership and capacity building across the African continent. In the near term, India should proactively forge comprehensive counter-terror cooperation with the AU (just as it has with other major partners like the US and the EU) and invest in building capacity to bolster the counter-terror infrastructure of individual African countries. Indian missions need to step up intelligence-gathering, with regard to the potential terror threats emanating from Africa.

Countries like the US and France have been especially proactive in their efforts to forge a long-term strategy to combat terrorism in Africa. The French Interior Minister Manuel Valls on November 15, 2013 announced that France would create a "regional homeland security envoy" role in Dakar to support the fight against terrorism in Africa's Sahel region.[8] In another important development, the US state department is said to be planning to declare the Nigerian Islamist militant group, Boko Haram, as a foreign terrorist organisation, which would entail US regulatory agencies blocking all business and financial transactions with Boko Haram. In a statement on October 15, 2014, the White House vowed that the US was working hard "to dismantle this murderous group," which had abducted hundreds of men, women, girls and boys, and killed 3,000 people in Nigeria. "President Obama has directed that the US government do everything it can to help the Nigerian government find and free the abducted girls and, more broadly, to combat Boko Haram in partnership with Nigeria, its neighbours, and other allies," the White House said.[9] While Western countries are engaged in the process of forging their individual and joint strategies to combat the scourge of terrorism in Africa, India needs to do more. Aligning with the West on Africa could be problematic due to historical baggage India's Western partners carry in the continent, but it makes pragmatic sense for India to enter into Africa-focused counter-terror cooperation with some Western countries with which it enjoys robust security cooperation, like the US and France.

India has projected itself as a preferred partner in the ongoing African resurgence and has pledged over $8 billion for a host of infrastructure projects. New Delhi is also planning to set up over 100 training institutes that seek to promote the rise of a middle class in Africa and provide the African youth opportunities for self-advancement. However, to translate the ideal of partnering African resurgence into reality, New Delhi needs to match its developmental and economic partnership with Africa with a well-thought out framework for deepening security and strategic cooperation with the continent. This should be one of the important outcomes flowing from the third India-Africa Forum Summit, which will be hosted by New Delhi in 2015.

NOTES

1. Brigadier General Jeffrey Marshall, EUCOM Engagement in Africa, briefing presented to the Conference on AFRICOM at Airlie House, Virginia, sponsored by the Department of Defense, September 23, 2007, p. 16.
2. Emily Mellgard, "Terrorism in Africa: An Inside Look At the 3 Most Dangerous African Terrorist Groups" http://mic.com/articles/66127/terrorism-in-africa-an-inside-look-at-the-3-most-dangerous-african-terrorist-groups (Accessed December 14, 2013).
3. Ibid.
4. Ibid.
5. Ibid.
6. "While World Watches ISIS, Boko Haram Declares Its Own Caliphate in Nigeria" http://www.nbcnews.com/storyline/missing-nigeria-schoolgirls/while-world-watches-isis-boko-haram-declares-its-own-caliphate-n202556 (Accessed December 15, 2014).
7. Yochi Dreazen, "Why Africa Is the New Terrorism Hub," *The Atlantic*, Sept 18, 2013 http://www.theatlantic.com/magazine/archive/2013/10/the-new-terrorist-training-ground/309446 (Accessed October 15, 2013).
8. "France to send envoy to Africa to lead anti-terror operations" at http://article.wn.com/view/2013/08/26/France_to_send_envoy_to_Africa_to_lead_antiterror_operations/ (Accessed October 15, 2014).
9. US dedicated to dismantling 'murderous' Boko Haram: White House; http://www.presstv.ir/detail/2014/10/14/382258/us-working-to-dismantle-boko-haram/ (Accessed October 15, 2014).

6

The Changing Natural Resources Profile of the West Indian Ocean Region: Implications for Maritime Security

Alex Benkenstein

The escalation of maritime violence off the Horn of Africa during the first decade of the 21st century has been met by an unprecedented level of international political and military cooperation, reflecting the strategic importance of the Indian Ocean to numerous regional and global powers. While incidents of piracy have decreased in recent years, these attacks have also been marked by greater sophistication and a wider geographic reach. Moreover, the expansion of the mineral and energy resource sectors in the West Indian Ocean will give rise to new challenges and vulnerabilities with regards to regional maritime security in the coming decade. The chapter provides an overview of the changing natural resources profile of the West Indian Ocean region with particular reference to offshore oil and gas, and the trade in minerals and energy resources. In the context of this changing natural resources profile, the chapter assesses the priorities for India-Africa maritime security cooperation in the coming decade.

Maritime Security: A Review of the International Response to Piracy

In the first decade of the 21st century incidents of piracy[1] increased significantly in the West Indian Ocean region, in the context of continued instability in Somalia and the increasing sophistication of Somali-based pirate action groups (PAGs). Piracy attacks off Somalia's coast had occurred during the 1990s, but after 2003-04 these earlier opportunistic and sporadic efforts were replaced by a more complex, efficient and profit-oriented business model, linked to Somali cartels, wealthy 'investors' within Somalia and the Somali diaspora, and international financial networks.[2]

The comprehensive international response to the rise of Somali piracy has underlined the importance of the West Indian Ocean region and sea lanes of communication to global commerce, energy security and regional stability. Three counter-piracy maritime forces, the European Union (Atalanta), NATO (Ocean Shield) and the Combined Maritime Forces (Combined Task Force 151), as well as naval counter-piracy missions from several individual states such as India, China, Indonesia, Japan, the Republic of Korea, Malaysia, Pakistan and Russia have cooperated in the West Indian Ocean.[3] China's involvement in anti-piracy activities represented the country's first patrolling mission outside the Pacific. During 2012 there were between 21 and 30 vessels from numerous nations engaged in east African counter-piracy efforts at any given time.[4]

Naval forces have escorted vessels travelling the waters off the Horn of Africa and the Internationally Recommended Transit Corridor in the Gulf of Aden, disrupted piracy attacks, arrested pirates and transferred them to national jurisdictions for prosecution, and supported states in the region in the development of counter-piracy capacity. Given the sheer scale of naval deployment in the region, the Shared Awareness and Deconfliction (SHADE) initiative was established in 2008 in order to assist in identifying redundancies in naval operations and identifying opportunities for collaboration. The SHADE meetings, for example, allowed Japan, China, India and later South Korea to coordinate naval escort deployments through the Escort Convoy Coordination initiative.

The United Nations Security Council (UNSC) and various United Nations agencies have been central actors in shaping the international response to Somali piracy. The UNSC has played a particularly important role in legitimising naval operations against Somali-based pirate groups, both within international waters and Somalia's territorial waters. The UNSC Resolution 1816 (2008) first allowed states to enter the territorial waters of Somalia for the purposes of repressing acts of piracy and armed robbery at sea. Resolution 1816 also called for information sharing and cooperation among states and interested organisations, including the International Maritime Organisation (IMO), as well as the provision of technical assistance to Somalia and nearby coastal states to ensure coastal and maritime security. A number of subsequent resolutions addressed various aspects of Somali-based piracy, particularly with regard to coordination of counter-piracy efforts, capacity building, information sharing and the need for legislative and judicial frameworks for the successful prosecution of detained pirates. Most recently, UNSC Resolution 2125 was passed in November 2013, reiterating the UNSC's condemnation of all acts of piracy committed at sea off the coast of Somalia, urging continued international cooperation in combating Somali piracy and calling upon Somali authorities to pass a complete set of anti-piracy laws without delay.

The Contact Group on Piracy off the Coast of Somalia (CGPCS) was developed in response to UNSC Resolution 1851 (2008), which called for the establishment of an international cooperation mechanism to coordinate international efforts at combating piracy off the coast of Somalia. The CGPCS meetings have been attended by representatives from at least 60 countries and observers from a large number of international and regional organisations, navies, industry and seafarer organisations and other non-state groups.[5] The CGPCS includes working groups tasked with military and operational coordination, capacity building, judicial issues, shipping self-awareness, public information related to piracy and financial flows related to piracy.

Other UN agencies involved in the response to Somali-based piracy include the United Nations Office on Drugs and Crime (UNODC), the IMO, the UN Food and Agriculture Organisation and the UN Political Office for Somalia. The UNODC established a counter piracy programme in 2009 through which it assists Kenya, Seychelles, Mauritius, Tanzania, Maldives and Somalia in strengthening law enforcement capabilities and improving prison conditions and capacity. The IMO, the United Nations specialised agency with responsibility for the safety and security of shipping and the prevention of marine pollution by ships, has worked closely with the shipping industry and other stakeholders in developing and promulgating best practices and codes of conduct on anti-piracy efforts. These include a range of recommendations related to the use of privately contracted armed security personnel by shipping companies. The IMO also convened a meeting in Djibouti in January 2009 which adopted the Djibouti Code of Conduct, a mechanism that seeks to coordinate a regional response by states bordering the West Indian Ocean, encompassing naval cooperation, information sharing and legislative reform. The IMO hosts the Djibouti Code of Conduct's Project Implementation Unit and also manages a trust fund that was set up as the central mechanism for funding the activities of the initiative.

The United Nations has further played an important role in facilitating the Kampala Process, a mechanism that seeks to support a coordinated anti-piracy response by Somalia's Transitional Federal Government, and the leadership of Puntland and Somaliland. One of the outcomes of the Kampala Process has been the development of a Somali Maritime Resource and Security Strategy in 2013, which was endorsed at the Somalia Conference in London on May 7, 2013 and the Third UAE Counter-Piracy Conference in September 2013.[6]

Efforts by the shipping industry, individually and through industry associations such as the World Shipping Council and the International Chamber of Shipping, have centred on collaboration with the IMO for the development of Best Management Practices for responding to Somali-based piracy. Some of the key recommendations included in this guidance are: increased speed for vessels travelling through high risk areas; the use of additional lookouts; employing physical barriers to avoid boarding; reporting of vessel position; and the use of a citadel to protect crew in the event of a boarding.[7]

The increasing use of privately contracted armed security personnel (PCASP) to protect vessels travelling in the West Indian Ocean has been a controversial aspect of the private sector's response to Somali-based piracy. The deployment of PCASP has expanded rapidly in recent years, despite a lack of governance frameworks to determine appropriate operating protocols related to the use of force. Numerous states with an economic and geostrategic interest in the West Indian Ocean have also expressed ambivalence with regard to the desirability of PCASP forces. The Indian Navy chief Admiral DK Joshi, for example, noted that there were close to 140 private security companies operating in the North Indian Ocean, with personnel that "shift between vessels at sea, without entering any port or coastal state regulated maritime territory", and "scores of ships operating as floating armouries, outside any coastal state jurisdiction".[8] India has been among the states calling for the development of an effective regulatory framework to govern the deployment of PCASP, preferably through the IMO.

The international response to Somali piracy has resulted in a significant decline in the reported incidents of piracy off the coast of Somalia. During the first nine months of 2012, 99 attacks took place, while during the first nine months of 2013 only 17 attacks occurred. The last large commercial vessel to have been hijacked and held for ransom by Somali pirates was the *MT Smyrni*, which was taken in May 2012; whereas not a single large commercial vessel was hijacked in the course of 2013. In a report to the United Nations Security Council, United Nations Secretary-General Ban Ki-Moon ascribed the decline in attacks to a range of measures, including: better intelligence- and information-sharing; targeted actions by the international naval presence to discourage and disrupt Somali pirates; increased application of IMO guidance and of the Best Management Practices for Protection against Somalia-based Piracy, developed by the shipping industry; and prosecution of suspected pirates and imprisonment of those convicted. The adoption of self-protection and situational awareness measures by commercial ships, including the deployment of privately contracted armed security personnel on board vessels and vessel protection detachments, are also believed to have contributed to the decrease in piracy attacks.[9]

The gains achieved by the extensive response to Somali piracy have been made despite increased shipping activity in the West Indian Ocean region, which has been driven in part by the growing role of the extractive sector in East Africa, as discussed in the following section.

The Emerging Resources Profile of the West Indian Ocean Region

The East African region is relatively unexplored with regards to potential mineral and energy resources. By 2010 a mere 600 exploration wells had been drilled in the region, compared to 14,000 and 20,000 in West and North Africa respectively.[10] The initial discovery of oil deposits in Uganda in 2006 and major gas finds off the coast of Mozambique and Tanzania in 2012, however, has precipitated significant exploration activities in the region. East Africa's energy potential has attracted investments from numerous major energy companies (ExxonMobil, Total and Royal Dutch Shell), large international exploration and production companies such as Anadarko, national oil companies (Statoil, Petrobras and Galp Energia) and small specialist firms such as Tullow and Cove Energy.[11] The finance manager at Kenya Ports Authority Patrick Nyoike, has commented that "activity in East Africa will increase significantly as world powers and international integrated oil players jockey for positions via both acquisitions and exploration".[12]

As exploration activity continues to increase it is likely that current estimates of total recoverable reserves will increase – for example, in September 2012 Uganda revised upwards its estimated oil reserves by 40 per cent from 2.5 to 3.5 billion barrels. While estimates of reserves vary widely and are subject to frequent revision, it has been estimated that about ten billion barrels of recoverable oil and gas could be found in East Africa's Rift Valley within the next decade: 3.5 billion barrels in Uganda, up to three billion each in Kenya and Tanzania, and at least half a billion barrels in Ethiopia.[13] With proven gas reserves of 127 trillion cubic feet (Tcf), Mozambique is expected to become the second-largest exporter of liquefied natural gas (LNG) by 2025, at which point the country may be exporting as much as 50 million tonnes per annum of LNG.[14]

It is likely to be some years before the East African region becomes a major energy exporter—significant production of Ugandan oil is expected by 2017, Mozambican gas by 2018 and Kenyan oil by 2018. Target dates for initial production are frequently postponed in light of operational challenges, legal disputes and governance issues. In Uganda, initial oil production was expected to commence by 2012, but disputes between investors and the Ugandan government on taxation, infrastructure and the establishment of refining capacity within Uganda has led to numerous delays in the development of the country's reserves. Despite the fact that it may be some years before the East African region becomes a major energy exporter, the growth in exploration activity and the expansion of transport infrastructure has already lead to a significant increase in marine traffic, in the form of exploration vessels, marine support vessels and rigs in the East African region.

The expansion of mining activities for a range of minerals in the region is also likely to have an impact on marine traffic. Mozambique's coal reserves, concentrated in Tete Province, have attracted major investments. Vale and Rio-Tinto (prior to Rio-Tinto's sale of its Mozambican assets to India-based International Coal Ventures Private Limited in 2014), had been exporting coal through the port of Beira via the Sena railway; however, Vale is investing $4.4 billion in a new railway in order to ship cargo from Tete Province to the deepwater port of Nacala. In 2013 the Mozambican government indicated that the Bangkok-based Italian-Thai Development Pcl had been selected to construct a 525km railway line from Tete to Macuse in Mozambique's Zambezia province as well as a port with a capacity of 25 million tonnes of cargo per year.[15] The port and rail infrastructure project is estimated to cost $5 billion and construction is to start in 2016. In Tanzania construction has already started on the $3 billion Mtwara Development Corridor, with China's Sichuan Hongda Company Limited the primary contractor. The Mtwara Port, which will be substantially expanded, lies close to the Mozambican border and Tanzania's own offshore gas reserves. The project includes the construction of an 860km railway linking iron ore and coal mines in Tanzania's interior with the coast, which will also facilitate trade between southern Tanzania and Malawi, Zambia and northern Mozambique. In 2013 China and Tanzania concluded a number of contracts related to the development of Bagomoyo port. The $11 billion project aims to establish Bagomoyo as the central trading hub in the East African region, with the capacity to handle 20 million containers a year, compared to Mombasa's current capacity of 600,000 and Dar es Salaam's 500,000.[16]

While the primary East African transport corridors (the Northern Corridor links Rwanda, Burundi, Uganda, Eastern DR Congo and Southern Sudan to the port of Mombasa, and the Central Corridor, linking

Uganda, Rwanda, Burundi and Tanzania through the port of Dar es Salaam) have been characterised by significant inefficiencies and slow cargo processing times, a number of investments are planned to improve the capacity and operating capability of both the Mombasa and Dar es Salaam ports, as well as the rail and road infrastructure linking these ports to the interior. In Kenya's northern region major developments are envisioned in the Lamu Port-South Sudan-Ethiopia Transport plan (LAPSETT), which would link the oil producing regions of South Sudan with emerging oil producers Uganda and Kenya via road and rail infrastructure as well as oil pipelines. While political will for the project remains strong, there are environmental and economic feasibility concerns, and it may be several years before the project is fully implemented.[17]

It has already been noted that large energy and infrastructure projects often become operational several years after initial target dates, nevertheless, an overview of recent discoveries of energy and mineral resources as well as current and planned infrastructure projects, provides clear evidence of the East African region becoming a major energy producer with greatly improved rail, road and port infrastructure to facilitate maritime trade. Therefore while considering the maritime security dimensions of the East African region, it is relevant to consider developments in the West African region as a more established energy producing region on the African continent.

West African Piracy: A portend for East Africa?

In 2012 West African piracy attacks for the first time exceeded those in Somalia, with 966 sailors attacked in West Africa, compared with 851 off the Somali coast.[18] The increasing frequency of piracy attacks in the Gulf of Guinea has received limited attention in past years as Somali-based piracy dominated media coverage and international anti-piracy efforts, yet more recently West African piracy gained prominence in the region and beyond. Piracy activities in the Gulf of Guinea differ from the Somali coast in that most vessels are attacked while at anchor, drifting or conducting ship-to-ship transfers of refined products cargo, while vessels in Somalia are attacked while they are at sea, with the objective of obtaining ransom payments for the release of the vessel and crew. In West Africa the target is often vessel cargo, in many cases high-value refined petroleum products.

These operations generally occur within 120 nautical miles from shore and are linked to organised criminal networks associated with land-based oil bunkering activities, purportedly often conducted in collaboration with corrupt officials within various government departments.[19] In 2012 seven incidents of oil theft by PAGS were reported, with between $2 million and $6 million of refined petroleum products stolen during each incident.[20]

While kidnapping for ransom is not as widespread as in the Somali region, such incidents have occurred. The Nigerian state of Bayelsa has been a particular hotspot for kidnapping. In April 2013 two Russian and two Ukranian oil workers were kidnapped. In February five crew members were kidnapped from an oil services ship off the coast of Bayelsa. There were also a number of pirate attacks in this region in late 2012, including the kidnapping of an Italian crew of an offshore supply vessel. In all, there were 31 incidents of piracy and armed robbery, including four hijackings, in the Gulf of Guinea during the first six months of 2013, according to the International Maritime Bureau (IMB). The IMB also noted the surge in kidnappings at sea and a wider range of ship types being targeted. Attacks off Nigeria accounted for 22 of the region's 31 incidents.[21]

The response to Somali piracy has been led by international institutions and various global powers, but there has been a stronger regional approach to addressing piracy in the Gulf of Guinea. West African heads of state gathered in Yaoundé, Cameroon, in June 2013 for a summit on maritime safety and security in the Gulf of Guinea. The summit agreed on the establishment of an Inter-regional Coordination Centre on Maritime Safety and Security for Central and West Africa to be headquartered in Yaoundé, and the adoption of a Code of Conduct on the repression of piracy, armed robbery and other illicit maritime activities in West and Central Africa. West African states are also currently developing an ECOWAS Integrated Maritime Strategy, aligned with the AIMS. Nigeria and Benin, the two West African states most affected by piracy, have signed a bilateral agreement for combined patrols. The Nigerian navy recently took delivery of four new patrol craft and has reported that 14 vessels have been apprehended in the past ten months while engaged directly or indirectly in acts of piracy.[22]

The emergence of East Africa's oil and gas sector raises the question of whether piracy operations in the Gulf of Guinea, which increasingly targets vessels associated with the region's petroleum sector, may serve as a window for future maritime security challenges in the West Indian Ocean region. It has already been emphasised that there are important differences in the mode of operations of the Gulf of Guinea and Somali pirates, which cautions against drawing a simplistic parallel between the two regions. The attacks in the Gulf of Guinea targeting petroleum and other high value cargo rely on a sophisticated underground economy that utilises infrastructure, trade channels and complex criminal networks that have been developed through years of illegal shore-based oil bunkering. The development of such a criminal economy on the East Coast of Africa in the medium term is unlikely, despite the highly 'corporatised' nature of Somali piracy.[23] More plausibly, Somali pirates will retain their existing strategies of targeting vessels for ransom with regard to the increased ship traffic. Indeed, in April 2012 the Tanzanian navy arrested pirates on a skiff near the Songsongo gas fields in the country's eastern region. The pirates had been using a former Sri Lankan fishing vessel as a mothership – which was also subsequently captured. Seven months earlier, Tanzania had arrested seven suspected Somali pirates following an attack on an oil and gas exploration ship operated by Brazilian petroleum company Petrobras off the coast of the country.[24]

While the primary *modus operandi* of Gulf of Guinea piracy is unlikely to emerge in East Africa over the coming decade, there is a risk that Somali pirates, like their counterparts in West Africa, will begin to resort to more sophisticated weaponry and more violent tactics in order to achieve their goals. Indeed, whereas in the West Indian Ocean no ship with private security detachment has been attacked to date, in the Gulf of Guinea vessels with armed guards have been successfully attacked. This has been ascribed to the more advanced weaponry employed in the Gulf of Guinea and the direct combat experience of those carrying out attacks, an outcome of the many years of regional and sub-regional conflicts that have occurred in the West African region and particularly within the Niger delta. Somali PAGS have demonstrated an ability to adapt to the changing security environment since piracy in the region first rose to prominence in 2005, for example, by using mother ships to extend the reach of PAGS as much as 1,500nm from shore.[25] Studies have shown how Somali-based piracy has evolved both in terms of broad strategies and operational tactics, emphasising the dynamic nature of piracy operations in the region.[26] Such adaptive strategies are likely to emerge within the changing dynamics of the West Indian Ocean region as trade in energy products, minerals and other commodities increase.

In order to understand the development of piracy activities in a given area it is essential to consider the wider socio-political dynamics of the region.[27] While pirate attacks may be coordinated and executed by organised criminal networks of considerable sophistication, the socio-political context of such activities is often rooted in the grievances of marginalised groups. Moreover, complex piracy activities such as those practiced in the West Indian Ocean and the Gulf of Guinea rely on an environment created by aweak or collapsed state, both in terms of the capability of the state to curtail violence and provide security, as well as its role in providing public services related to health, infrastructure, an equitable distribution of state resources and the fulfilment of other developmental roles. Piracy is thus an ambiguous composite of 'commercial' and political motivations. In a report to the UNSC, UN Secretary General Ban Ki-Moon observed that "the issue of piracy and armed robbery at sea off the coast of Somalia will be resolved only through an integrated approach that addresses the conflict, lack of governance and absence of sustainable livelihoods on land in Somalia."[28] This perspective has important implications for India-Africa maritime security cooperation in the Indian Ocean region.

Implications for India-Africa Maritime Security Cooperation

Over the past decade India's conceptualisation of its geostrategic role in the Indian Ocean region has achieved greater clarity and focus. Addressing the Combined Services Conference in 2004, India's Prime Minister Manmohan Singh emphasised that 'our strategic footprint covers...to the far reaches of the Indian Ocean. Awareness of this reality should inform and animate our strategic thinking and defence planning".[29] This message has been echoed by India's political and military leadership at a number of forums, and has informed a concerted effort to grow the capabilities of the Indian navy. In 2012 the Indian defence minister A.K. Antony, in his address to the Naval Chiefs Conference said that "India's strategic location in the Indian Ocean and the professional capability of our Navy bestows upon us a natural ability to play a leading role in ensuring peace and stability in the Indian Ocean Region".[30] The development of this thinking is also reflected in the move from a defensive and limited coastal naval paradigm expressed in the 1998 *Maritime and Military Strategy for India 1989-2014*, to the more assertive role premised on an oceanic focus and a clear leadership role in the region as stated in the 2004 *Indian Maritime Doctrine* and particularly the 2007 *India's Maritime Military Strategy*. India's military strategy recognises the importance of keeping Indian Ocean sea lanes of communication open, due in no small part to the importance of international trade to India's continuing economic growth and energy security. Addressing piracy as a threat to trade and regional order therefore aligns with India's strategic imperatives.

Since 2008 India has played an important role in combating Somali-based piracy, particularly through its role in escorting vessels in the Gulf of Aden, cooperation with information-sharing initiatives such as SHADE and other initiatives such as the Indian Ocean Naval Symposium, and through bilateral agreements and cooperation with East African states such as Mozambique. Importantly, India has also played a key diplomatic role in promoting a comprehensive and coordinated response to Somali piracy, including through lobbying for action through the United Nations Security Council. Although incidents of pirate attacks have decreased dramatically in the West Indian Ocean, the problem of Somali piracy cannot be resolved to any significant extent without resolving the issue of the lack of security and governance in Somalia itself. Such 'land-based' solutions require ongoing support for the United Nations and African Union efforts to bolster the Somali government, as well as efforts to address the international criminal networks and financial flows that underpin the activities of PAGs in the region. Such initiatives are particularly important given that the high level of naval deployment by various international actors in the Gulf of Aden region is widely considered to be financially unsustainable in the long term. Moreover, piracy operations can be relatively easily re-established after a period of inactivity unless the broader enabling conditions that contribute to these activities are addressed.

As the extraction, refining and transportation infrastructure is developed to service East Africa's oil and gas sector, there is an increased risk that this infrastructure may be targeted by marginalised sections of society, potentially mobilised to protest against environmental degradation and/or the inequitable distribution of revenues generated by natural resource sectors. United Nations Secretary-General Ban Ki-Moon has warned the UNSC that al Shabaab forces have increasingly turned from conventional military engagement to guerrilla warfare, including attacks on non-military and commercial targets, as evidenced in the Westgate Shopping Mall in Kenya in September 2013. The recent resurgence of violence in Mozambique by RENAMO forces raises concerns not only with regard to domestic stability; but also the potential of such conflicts, fuelled by perceptions of political and economic marginalisation, to threaten international commercial and security interests. Following the Mumbai terrorist attacks of November 2008 India focused on increasing its maritime domain awareness, coordination and response capability for near-shore security, particularly port security. These lessons are particularly valuable for the East African region as it expands its port infrastructure and shipping activity.

Piracy operations have undeniably come under growing pressure in recent years both from conventional military responses, private security personnel and the range of diplomatic and governance related anti-piracy initiatives outlined in this chapter. Attempted attacks continue to occur, however, providing evidence that the networks, capital and crews required for such attacks remain largely in place. The coordinated efforts of various navies in the north Indian Ocean have increased the risk of capture and the costs of engaging in piracy, but until "effective political authority and improved economic opportunities permanently alter the cost-benefit calculations of Somali pirates, the underlying incentives driving Somali piracy will remain unchanged, necessitating extensive and indefinite naval operations".[31] International actors, including India, therefore must continue their engagement in addressing the root causes of piracy operations in the region.

Conclusion

It is an oft repeated axiom that piracy must be defeated on land, rather than on the ocean. Similarly, maritime security considerations are shaped by political, economic and social dynamics within the societies where pirates are based. As the resource sectors of the East African region are further developed, it is likely that the distinctions between criminal, profit-driven piracy and violent, politically motivated opposition to regional authorities may become increasingly blurred. It has been argued that the Somali piracy 'business model' has been fundamentally undermined by the cooperative efforts of numerous navies, the increasing role of private security firms and the successes of land-based Kenyan military operations in Somalia. Yet, the ability of coordinated and sophisticated groups to carry out high-profile attacks on vulnerable targets will remain, especially in the context of weak states with limited ability to secure their land-based and maritime domains. Maritime security cooperation between India and Africa therefore must respond to a broader range of governance concerns that include more conventional approaches such as intelligence sharing, joint naval operations and even naval capacity building.

NOTES

1. It should be noted that, according to international law and the definition of piracy provided by the United Nations Convention on the Law of the Sea (UNCLOS), the term "piracy" relates only to criminal acts committed on the high seas; when such acts are perpetrated within a state's territorial waters they are referred to as armed robbery at sea. This article, however, employs the wider definition of piracy formulated by the International Maritime Bureau which includes criminal acts committed both on the high seas and within territorial waters – "piracy" should therefore be read as "piracy and armed robbery at sea".
2. D. Guilfoyle, "Somali Pirates as Agents of Change in International Law-making and Organization", *Cambridge Journal of International Comparative Law,* 1(3), 2013, pp. 81-106.
3. United Nations Security Council, "Report of the Secretary-General on the situation with respect to piracy and armed robbery at sea off the coast of Somalia", 21 October 2013, S/2013/623, p.9.
4. K. Hurlburt, *The Human Cost of Maritime Piracy 2012,* Oceans Beyond Piracy, at http://oceansbeyondpiracy.org/publications/human-cost-maritime-piracy-2012 (Accessed on October 7, 2013), p.13.
5. "An Interactive Guide to International Efforts to Address Piracy off the Coast of Activity", Oceans Beyond Piracy at http://oceansbeyondpiracy.org/matrix/activity/contact-group-piracy-coast-somalia-cgpcs (Accessed October 15, 2013)
6. United States Department of State, "Contact Group on Piracy off the Coast of Somalia: Quarterly Report", at http://www.state.gov/t/pm/rls/fs/2013/212140.htm (Accessed on January 12, 2014)
7. http://internationallawandpractice.ncbar.org/newsletters/internationallawoct2012/modernpiracy#sthash.KU8UWjOw.dpuf
8. "Floating Armories, Pvt Armed Guards Worry Navy", *StratPost,* December 6, 2013, at

http://www.stratpost.com/floating-armories-pvt-armed-guards-worry-navy (Accessed on January 25, 2014)
9. United Nations Security Council. *Report of the Secretary-General on the situation with respect to piracy and armed robbery at sea off the coast of Somalia*, 21 October 2013, S/2013/623, p.12.
10. Control Risks, *A New frontier: Oil and gas in East Africa*, 2012, p.1.
11. A. Ketron, "The Long Arm: The Impact of Modern Piracy", at http://www.trademarksa.org/news/oil-and-gas-discoveries-make-east-africa-rich-hunting-ground-global-explorers (Accessed on October 15, 2013)
12. "Oil and gas discoveries make East Africa rich hunting ground for global explorers", *Business Daily Africa* 2012, at http://www.mpakasi.com/?section=news&page=energy-mining&article=oil-and-gas-discoveries-make-east-africa-a-rich-hunting-ground-for-global-explorers&mode=print&pdf=true&downloadPdf=true&ru=%2Fnews%2Fenergy-mining%2Foil-and-gas-discoveries-make-east-africa-a-rich-hunting-ground-for-global-explorers%2F (Accessed on October 20 2013)
13. L. Diamond and J. Mosbacher, "Petroleum to the People: Africa's Coming Resource Curse – and How to Avoid It", *Foreign Affairs,* September/October 2013.
14. Pricewaterhouse Coopers, "From Promise to Performance: Africa Oil & Gas Review", 2013, at http://www.pwc.co.za/en_ZA/za/assets/pdf/africa-oil-and-gas-review-2013.pdf (Accessed on October 7 2013)
15. Reuters, "Mozambique picks Thai firm to build coal railway, port", 27 November 2013, at http://lta.reuters.com/article/marketsNews/idLTAL5N0JC24G20131127 (Accessed on 15 January 2013)
16. "China, Tanzania's Biggest Development Partner", *The East African*, at http://www.theeastafrican.co.ke/news/China—Tanzania-biggest-development-partner-/-/2558/2160314/-/item/0/-/2el6ijz/-/index.html (Accessed on 20 January 2014)
17. Reuters, "Grand Kenya Port Plan Faces Headwinds Despite Oil Finds", at http://www.reuters.com/article/2013/08/30/us-kenya-port-analysis-idUSBRE97T0CM20130830 (Accessed on January 29, 2014)
18. K, Hurlburt, n.4.
19. P.K. Ghosh, "Waiting to Explode: Piracy in the Gulf of Guinea", *Observer Research Foundation Occasional Paper* No.46, at http://orfonline.org/cms/sites/orfonline/modules/occasionalpaper/OccasionalPaperList.html (Accessed on October 2013).
20. K. Hurlburt, n.4.
21. Nairaland Forum, "Oil, Gas Industry's Top 5 Kidnapping Hotspots", at http://www.nairaland.com/1413394/oil-gas-industrys-top-5 (Accessed on November 12, 2013)
22. A. Benkenstein, "Gulf of Guinea: The new flashpoint of Piracy in Africa?", 16 December 2013, at http://www.saiia.org.za/opinion-analysis/gulf-of-guinea-the-new-flashpoint-of-piracy-in-africa (Accessed on 15 January, 2013)
23. P.K. Ghosh, "Somalian Piracy: An Alternative Perspective", *Observer Research Foundation Occasional Paper,* No.16, September 2010.
24. Reuters, "Tanzania arrests five suspected pirates near gas fields", 20 April 2012, at http://www.defenceweb.co.za/index.php?option=com_content&view=article&id=25119:tanzania-arrests-five-suspected-pirates-near-gas-fields&catid=51:Sea&Itemid=106 (Accessed on October 5, 2013)
25. P.K. Ghosh, "Waiting to Explode: Piracy in the Gulf of Guinea", *Observer Research Foundation Occasional Paper* No.46, at http://orfonline.org/cms/sites/orfonline/modules/occasionalpaper/OccasionalPaperList.html (Accessed on October 2013).

26. K. Sorenson and J.J. Widen, "Irregular Warfare and Tactical Changes: The Case of Somali Piracy", *Terrorism and* Political *Violence*, 26 (3) 2014, pp.1-20.
27. P.K. Ghosh, n.23.
28. UN Political Office for Somalia, "Somalia and Piracy", at http://unpos.unmissions.org/Default.aspx?tabid=9742&language=en-US (Accessed on October 24, 2013)
29. Quoted in David Scott "India's Strategy for the Indian Ocean Region", *Journal of Strategic Studies*, 36(4), 2013 pp. 484-511.
30. Ibid
31. Thomas Keating, "The Political Economy of Somali Piracy", *SAIS Review*, 31(1), Winter-Spring 2013, pp. 185-191.

7

India's Coastal Security: Sharing Best Practices with African Nations

Vijay Sakhuja

Coastal spaces represent both promise and peril. At one end of the spectrum, they provide the muscle for economic growth and development, and on the other end these spaces are the focal points of illegal activity. Lack of governance and an ineffective security apparatus in the coastal areas has created conditions that favour the growth of terrorism, piracy and other illegal activities. Further, terrorism 'from the sea' is a reality as demonstrated by the Mumbai terror attacks.

Post the Mumbai terror attacks in 2008, India undertook a major overhaul of its coastal security apparatus which involved: the restructuring of security organisations; infrastructure development to bridge the gaps in maritime surveillance and reconnaissance; training of personnel; technological improvements; and increasing the number of stakeholders. Further, India initiated a dialogue with some of its maritime neighbours to address transnational maritime threats and challenges, by taking a number of initiatives such as bilateral naval exercises, regular ship visits, training, transfer of naval hardware and sharing of intelligence. At the multilateral level, i.e. IORA and the IONS, it adopted a proactive approach and laid greater stress on cooperative maritime security.

This paper details the initiatives undertaken by the Indian government to address issues of coastal security. It is hoped, that this paper, will enable African states to identify best security practices to enhance their maritime security.

Mumbai Terror Attacks

Ten members of the Pakistan based terror outfit the Lashkar-e-Taiba (LeT) carried out the 2008 Mumbai terror attacks. They embarked from Karachi on three boats and later hijacked the *Kuber* an Indian fishing off Porbandar, on the Gujarat coast and landed on unsecured waterfronts in south Mumbai. Their targets included two prestigious hotels, a railway station and a local Jewish congregation place killing nearly 138 people including 28 foreigners. Of the 10 terrorists, one was captured alive and his subsequent interrogation helped to unravel the entire plan of action including the identity of the masterminds behind the attacks in Mumbai.

The operation was meticulously planned by the perpetrators and the attackers were well trained. They were equipped with satellite telephones to receive guidance from their advisors in Pakistan, and made expert use of Global Positioning System (GPS) for navigation, had good knowledge of the landing points in south Mumbai and were also highly motivated. These attacks highlighted the vulnerability of India's maritime security particularly on its west coast that is contiguous with Pakistan.

The attacks highlighted that 'terrorism from the sea' was a reality, in view of the fact that the Indian establishment had thus far been focussing on land based terrorism, both by external and internal outfits. The attacks also led to the realisation that maritime infrastructure is vulnerable to attacks from the surface, sub-surface and air, by means of swimmers, divers, fast motor boats, sub surface vessels and floating wreckage. The use of aircraft for attacks as witnessed during the 9/11 attacks in the US was also taken into account as was the use of mini-submarines and other submersible platforms by drug lords in Colombia .

Post Mumbai Attack Security Apparatus

Post the Mumbai terror attacks, the Indian government set up the National Investigative Agency (NIA) to counter fight terrorism-related crimes, established a Coastal Command (CC) for the security of the coastline and Maritime Defence Zones (MDZ) along India's coastline and island territories. Other initiatives included: the mandatory registration of fishing boats; issue of biometric identity cards to fishermen; formation of state maritime boards; designation of shipping lanes in ports; survey and monitoring of landing points along the coast.[1] It was also decided to set up coastal radar stations to enhance coastal surveillance. Forty six such stations have been established in Phase 1 of the exercise; and another 38 radar stations are planned during Phase II. According to Vice Admiral MP Muralidharan, Director General, Indian Coast Guard (ICG): "We have a chain of radar stations that have been set up for the entire coastal security network which will be ready at the end of this year along the mainland and early next year it will be ready in our island territories."[2]

At another level, the Indian Coast Guard is being modernised and equipped to manage India's coastal security more efficiently. A variety of ships and shore based surveillance assets have been acquired and others are in the pipeline. The DG ICG recently said that the Coast Guard would have a 150-ships and over l00 aircraft by 2018 and that "as of today, there are over 100 ships in various stages of construction both at the defence public shipyards and private shipyards across the country."

There are plans to enact a law on coastal security and the Indian navy chief has been quoted as saying that: "We are constantly upgrading the infrastructure, and working towards augmentation of resources. A coastal security bill has also been drafted…The coastal security bill will further enhance multiple agency coordination and centre-state coordination,"[3]

Private Security Agencies

The rising graph of sea piracy off Somalia has sparked off commercial activities such as escort companies, and private security agencies who supply trained personnel for onboard security duties. The maritime world has seen an exponential rise in the number of private security agencies that offer a variety of services at sea. According to the "*Economic Cost of Somali Piracy 2012* (ECoP 2012)" a report commissioned by Oceans Beyond Piracy (OBP), a project of the One Earth Future Foundation (OEF):

> …most pronounced increase in the cost of piracy came as a result of the

> increased number of armed guards used to protect merchant vessels transiting the HRA. Between US$ 1.15 and US$ 1.53 billion was spent on armed guards in 2012. In 2011 that figure was US$ 530.6 million. The observed increase comes as the result of an increased proportion of ships employing armed guards (30 per cent in 2011 and at least 50 per cent in 2012) as well as a revised estimate of the number of commercial transits through the HRA each year. Controlling for that latter methodological factor, the cost of armed guards increased 79.7 per cent in 2012.[4]

In India too, the private security sector is booming with Indian companies and private individuals spending nearly $ 5 billion annually on private security guards, cameras and surveillance equipment, bodyguards, etc. Post the Mumbai attacks this industry has grown at nearly 20 per cent annually and is expected to touch $ 10 billion over the next five years.[5] The International Maritime Organisation (IMO) too has expressed concerns that these measures could:

> ...result in escalation of violence at sea, stringent local regulations during ports calls, and casualties due to inadvertent or accidental firing and therefore such measures were not in the interest of international shipping which is highly sensitive to risks and dangers arising from even low level combat.[6]

The Indian government has not allowed private security guards on Indian flagged vessels.

Perhaps one of the important reasons against posting private security armed guards on board ships are the laws of the coastal state relating to of weapons onboard ships. In this context, two incidents in India waters merit attention.

In the first case, *MV Enrica Lexie* spotted a fast moving vessel 33 miles south-west of the coast of India on its radar and calculated that it was on a collision course with the vessel. The Italian marines deployed on board as private security guards fired warning shots across the bows of the fishing boat, but four shots hit the vessel killing two fishermen. The marines were arrested and the matter is currently pending before the court.

The second is the case of *MV Seaman Guard Ohio*. The case of this Sierra Leone flagged vessel owned by the US based company AdvanFort is intriguing and showcases the rise of 'private navies'. The vessel, with 35 maritime security contractors and crew, was intercepted in Indian waters. However, the master of the vessel claimed that at the time of interception, the vessel was in international waters and that, "Their weapons and ammunition were locked and sealed in storage throughout their stay on the ship." Further, "The weapons and ammunition—all of which were purchased in the UK—were authorised and licenced with the appropriate authorities and governing bodies". The bail petition to the apprehended crew is pending before the High Court of Madurai in India.

The Indian navy is concerned about these unregulated 'floating armouries' and "this has very serious security implications for us including the infiltration of terrorists." The navy chief has observed that:

> If there are unregulated arms and ammunition on a vessel, the existence of weapons is not known as also where guards are transferring them and this could lead to such a situation on anybody's soil.[7]

Perhaps what merits the attention of the East African Indian Ocean littorals is the Indian Navy chief's observation that:

> There are close to 140 private security companies operating in North Indian Ocean, which hire out privately contracted armed security personnel. These personnel shift between vessels at sea, without entering any port or coastal state regulated maritime territory.[8]

According to Article 27 of the 1982 UNCLOS it is the coastal states' responsibility to ...exercise its criminal jurisdiction over a foreign flagged vessel in certain exceptional circumstances, including where the consequences of the crime extend to the coastal state, and where the crime is of a kind to disturb the peace of the country, or the good order of the territorial sea.[9]

The above incidents clearly show that in both these cases India exercised its jurisdiction under the 1982 UNCLOS and national legislation which needs to be understood by the private security agencies.

Indian guidelines for positioning armed guards onboard merchant ships and employing/embarking privately contracted armed security personnel on board merchant ships transiting through high-risk piracy prone areas are based on the May 2011, the Maritime Safety Committee (MSC) of the International Maritime Organisation (IMO) 'interim' guidelines (MSC.1/ Circ. 1405 &1406) relating to engaging private maritime security companies (PMSC) Importantly, the Indian guidelines 'do not endorse the use of armed guards on merchant ships'.

Trilateral Maritime Security Cooperation: India, Maldives and Sri Lanka

The trilateral maritime security cooperation between India, Maldives and Sri Lanka is a good example of a possible multilateral approach towards maintaining maritime order in the southern Arabian Sea. At the functional–operational level, the Indian navy has engaged both the Maldives and Sri Lankan navies through bilateral naval exercises, regular ship visits, training, transfer of naval hardware and sharing of intelligence.

As noted earlier, post the 2008 Mumbai terror attacks, the Indian maritime security organisations have been revamped with the establishment of the Coastal Command and setting up of Joint Operation Centres, are also in the process of acquiring cutting edge technologies to enhance littoral security. Sri Lanka has also a degree of naval capability that was very effectively used to fight the LTTE but still lacks surveillance and response capability on the high seas. The Maldives maritime forces are essentially constabulary in nature and lack combat capability. Further, by all estimates, the current security architecture of Sri Lanka and Maldives is not robust enough to deter, detect and defeat a challenger partly due to lack of capabilities.

Notwithstanding the wide technological gaps between the three navies, they have carried out maritime exercises code-named *Exercise Dosti* and attempted to develop interoperability. Besides gaining operational experience, these engagements have been instrumental in enhancing mutual trust and confidence. Significantly, Dosti is a bi-annual exercise which was first held in 1991 with the objective of strengthening cooperation between the Coast Guards of India and Maldives. In its 20th year, the Sri Lankan Coast Guard joined in and it has now become a trilateral engagement.[10]

Enhancing Security through Best Practices and Solutions

Technological Solutions

(a) Unmanned aviation platforms such as the UAVs are capable of providing real or near-real time tactical pictures of sea areas, monitor maritime activity, and also possess the capability to destroy suspected targets. These would need to be integrated with the maritime security architectures of the contiguous states.

(b) Aerostats and balloons can carry a variety of payloads including radar, communication systems and other sensors.

(c) The low-cost model of Automatic Identification System (AIS) developed by the Indian Space Research Organisation (ISRO) is a cost effective solution for enhancing monitoring of traffic at sea.

(d) Compulsory AIS on smaller vessels, mandatory registration of all fishing vessels and biometric identification cards given by the three partners can enhance trilateral cooperation.

Operational Efficiency

(a) Operational interoperability with neighbouring navies would result in enhanced understanding, foster mutual trust and co-ordination among the partners.

(b) A common doctrine and SOPs for greater cooperation and improving communications for interoperability.

(c) Education of coastal communities including fishermen of the dangers lurking in the littorals and promoting the idea of them being important stakeholders in the surveillance network is critical.

Capacity Building

(a) As part of capacity building, the partners can enhance regional capacity through training exercises and the Indian Coast Guard can take the lead in this aspect.

(b) Indian navy can play an active role in promoting further cooperation with African navies by strengthening existing relationships, expanding training and education assistance and help develop a regional maritime information database.

(c) Cooperation to improve surveillance and enforcement of fisheries in coastal areas which can be expanded to Exclusive Economic Zones.

(d) Develop cooperative mechanisms for search and rescue, assistance to the fishing community and disaster relief activities.

Concluding Remarks

It is an acknowledged fact that maritime security is best addressed by extending the defence perimeter further out into the sea and securing the coastal areas. This can be best achieved through maritime awareness, technological solutions and cooperative structures.

Further, maritime multilateralism will enable nations to address non-traditional threats and challenges at sea. The Indian Ocean Rim Association of Regional Cooperation (IOR-ARC), now rechristened as the Indian Ocean Rim Association (IORA) and the Indian Ocean naval symposium (IONS) a pan Indian Ocean security apparatus started in 2008, can play an important role in enhancing security in the Indian Ocean. Interestingly, Somali piracy in the Gulf of Aden had offered a unique opportunity to IORA to take note of security issues; however it did not make any significant efforts to bring the regional countries together to address this menace.

A host of multilateral initiatives such as the Shared Awareness and Deconfliction (SHADE), the Contact Group for Piracy off the Coast of Somalia (CGPCS), the Djibouti Code of Conduct (DCoC) and the Internationally Recommended Transit Corridor (IRTC), have mushroomed to address the issue of Somali piracy, but a sub-regional approach to address common maritime security concerns should be priority for African countries.

NOTES

1. "Antony Reviews Coastal Security", Press Information Bureau, Government of India, Ministry of Defence November 12, 2013.
2. "India's Coastal Radar Chain by this Year-End". http://www.defencenow.com/news/530/indias-coastal-radar-chain-by-this-year-end.html (Accessed December 1, 2013).
3. "Floating armouries risk 26/11-type attacks: Navy Chief DK Joshi", http://zeenews.india.com/news/nation/navy-chief-warns-unregulated-private-armoury-ships-can-risk-another-26/11_894052.html (Accessed December 4, 2013).

4. "Total Cost of Piracy: $ 5.7 billion to $6.1 billion". http://www.marinelog.com/index.php?option=com_k2&view=item&id=3863:total-cost-of-piracy-$57-billion-to-$61-billion&Itemid=107 (Accessed December 1, 2013).
5. Amy Kazmin and Avantika Chilkoti. "Mumbai terror attacks anniversary raises India security doubts", *Financial Times* [India], November 25, 2013.
6. Vijay Sakhuja. "Securing India's Littorals," *Journal of Defence Studies*, 3(2), April 2009, pp. 157-171.
7. "Floating armouries risk 26/11-type attacks: Navy Chief DK Joshi", http://zeenews.india.com/news/nation/navy-chief-warns-unregulated-private-armoury-ships-can-risk-another-26/11_894052.html (Accessed December 4, 2013).
8. "Navy sounds alarm on 'floating armouries", *The Times of India*, 4 December 2013.
9. For more details see *United Nations Convention on the Law of the Sea* United Nations, pp. 33-34.
10. "India, Sri Lanka and Maldives conduct joint Coast Guard exercise – DOSTI XI". http://voiceof.india.com/features/india-sri-lanka-and-maldives-conduct-joint-coast-guard-exercise-dosti-xi/2523 (Accessed December 1, 2013).

8

Enhancing India-Africa Maritime Security Cooperation

Abhijit Singh

Among the recent changes in India's strategic thinking, has been a partial reorientation of its maritime outlook towards Africa. With a growing economic engagement in the African continent, New Delhi has sought to gradually expand its sphere of influence in the Western Indian Ocean. The proactive maritime outreach on India's western flank has resulted in noteworthy endeavours in the small-island states of Mauritius and Seychelles, with some initiatives even involving continental Africa.

For over a decade now, Africa has figured prominently in India's energy security discussions. With its attention focused squarely on Africa's oil and minerals, however, India's evolving ties in Africa have largely been in the nature of 'resource-based' relationships—intended to feed a booming domestic demand for energy. New Delhi's interest in Nigeria, for instance, is driven by the fact that the latter has been India's top oil supplier in Africa, accounting for a significant part of Indian trade with the continent.[1] India's policies have also been influenced by the strong market for India's manufactured goods in Africa.

India's interest in maritime security in Africa, however, remains essentially focused on the continent's east coast. Since 2008, the primary driver of India's security initiative in Africa has been piracy off Somalia.[2] While the Indian navy has been making significant contributions to anti-piracy operations in the Western Indian Ocean, it has played a much smaller role in maritime security efforts in Africa. To be sure, there has been a realisation on India's part that in order to make a substantive contribution to securing Africa's maritime environs, the nature of its engagement will need to go beyond anti-piracy assistance in Somalia, and the mere protection of 'security of the sea lines of communication' (SLOCs) in the Eastern Indian Ocean.

Even so, progress in developing a coherent and viable plan of action, has been slow. Both Africa and India have found it difficult to change their regional maritime mind-set and have made halting efforts towards developing an effective maritime collaboration. There is now an emerging view among Indian analysts that India's growing maritime influence, and rising African expectations relating to increased commitment by partner states in support of Africa's regional maritime security, has made it imperative for the Indian navy to enhance its involvement in Africa's coastal security. This paper outlines the efforts undertaken so far by both India and Africa for improving their maritime collaboration, and delineates potential areas of cooperation.

India's Maritime Realities

As the preponderant maritime power in South Asia, India today faces three realities. First, the changing global distribution of power has led to the deepening of existing divisions amongst the world's leading nations, thereby complicating the management of the global maritime commons. There is an increased contestation between 'regional' and 'extra-regional' forces on the governance of maritime spaces. Second, the pressures on the defence budget have resulted in the downsizing of armed forces thereby restricting the maritime powers' ability to deliver public goods in the maritime domain. This has translated into a 'wait-and-watch' approach to distant threats, while letting friendly nations bear more of the costs for their own defence. Lastly, there has been an expansion of the interests and involvement of small littoral states in maritime security matters. India, despite an adverse economic environment, cannot afford to be seen as a reluctant participant in the security of the Indian Ocean Region.[3] Not only must it act in the maritime domain, its contribution to regional security must be seen to be 'prompt' and 'proactive'.

In many ways, India's three nautical dilemmas are reflected in its engagement in Africa and the Southern Indian Ocean, where huge maritime commons are ungoverned and unregulated. India does not have the resources and force-levels to be a regular security provider in this region, but still feels obliged to act, especially since regional states lack maritime capacity to provide their own security.

Africa's Maritime Imperatives

India's response is driven mainly by Africa's rising stakes in the maritime domain. The continent's significant maritime proportions are reflected in the fact, that out of its 54 countries, 38 are either coastal or island states with a vast coast line of 30,725 km. More significantly, 90 percent of the continent's total imports and exports are carried by sea. If the illegal market in military arms and logged forest products is taken into account, Africa has a maritime economy that is estimated at a trillion dollars a year, representing a staggering 90 percent of its overall commerce.[4]

Ironically enough, it is only over the past few years that Africa (as a collective entity) has come to realise the importance of its maritime security. With a booming mining and oil industry, Africa has been at the centre of global attention that has resulted in a number of energy-hungry countries like China and India gravitate towards its shores. The increased resource extraction has led to an exponential increase in sea traffic, and a corresponding growth in the rate of maritime crime.

Many African states, however, lack the capacity to ensure the security of their declared maritime zones. This has also resulted in a vast illegal capture of maritime resources giving rise to a clamour for better maritime governance. To complicate matters further, interstate maritime borders have remained poorly defined, raising the possibility of future maritime border disputes.

The high incidence of Somali piracy between 2008 and 2011 brought the issue of African maritime security to the world's attention. The seriousness of the crisis is reflected by a much deeper problem—a near-absence of a maritime governance framework and the lack of a harmonising vision for an African maritime economy.[5] The plethora of threats confronting coastal African states today include illegal fishing, smuggling, narcotics smuggling, illegal immigration and pollution. Every unlawful activity in African waters has a uniquely debilitating effect on the regional economy.

Africa's maritime resource management problems are exemplified by its unregulated fishing sector. A vast majority of the continent's rapidly growing population depends on fish, both inland and coastal, for its protein. Yet, there is rampant illegal fishing which translates into massive losses for the regional maritime economy. It highlights the lack of policing and management infrastructure within individual states that precludes a robust response to the challenge. While many regional initiatives have been undertaken to address the challenges, Africa's need for maritime governance stands out as being pressing and urgent.

Africa's Maritime Security

For long, Africa had been indifferent towards its own maritime security. The reason for its disinterest in the administration of its maritime zones was the absence of naval capabilities among African states, which made naval warfare or the military escalation of maritime disputes a remote prospect. The situation changed significantly in 2005, when a 'piracy momentum' resulted in some path-breaking maritime security cooperation.[6] In the years since, maritime security in Africa has been driven by the economic interests of the coastal states. Today, the challenges faced by African states with regard to the governance of their maritime zones reveal the security assistance they seek[7]:

(a) Lack of appropriate frameworks for the delimitation of the maritime zones.
(b) Lack of appropriate policy, legal and institutional frameworks for governance of the maritime zones.
(c) Inadequate training facilities and institutions to develop a pool of competent human resources for the governance process.
(d) Exploration of, and research on marine resources.

(e) Marine pollution from land-based and ship-based sources.
(f) Illegal, unreported and unregulated (IUU) fishing from distant water fishing nation vessels.
(g) Piracy and hostage taking
(h) Inadequate disaster preparedness to deal with maritime searches
(i) Illegal immigration
(j) Drug trafficking
(k) Smuggling of contraband goods and arms
(l) Inadequate port security

Africa's Maritime Governance

The earliest African attempt to address the issue of maritime security goes back to 1995, when the SADC set up a Standing Maritime Committee (SMC) as a sub-body of the Interstate Defence and Security Committee (ISDSC). A few years later, maritime terrorism in East Africa led to a type of naval engagement in the form of the US led Combined Maritime Forces patrolling the Eastern Indian Ocean.[8]

For many years, the SMC coordinated naval forces of SADC members. Since 2011, it has been actively formulating a regional anti-piracy strategy.[9] The strategy proposes the joint procurement of naval vessels and the creation of Maritime Domain Awareness (MDA) centres to facilitate information sharing on maritime security incidents and maritime traffic. The strategy also supports the revision of legal frameworks to apprehend and prosecute pirates and to work towards the ratification of international maritime treaties. A task force, comprising of navy commanders from Tanzania, Mozambique and South Africa was formed to lead the implementation of this initiative.

In 2005, the IGAD decided to coordinate its strategies and action plans to address the challenge of piracy. Maritime security issues, notably Somali piracy, smuggling as well as illegal fishing and waste dumping were recurrent themes in IGAD's various meeting agendas. Maritime security was part of the agenda of IGAD's Capacity Building Programme against Terrorism (ICPAT). IGAD also took up the task of drafting a "Somalia Inland Action Plan to counter and prevent Piracy 2010-2015."[10]

The first Sea Power for Africa Symposium (SPAS) was held under the auspices of the AU in 2005. It has since become one of the major forums for deliberation with further meetings being held in 2006, 2009 and 2011. It has also widened its base to include representatives from all African states and major international organisations as well as civil authorities, such as port facility, transport industry, and academia.

What is unique about the SPAS's management model is, that it is based on the resolutions passed at the end of each SPAS, which bind each of the attendees to achieve stated maritime objectives within a stipulated time frame.[11] The extensive resolutions range from co-operation issues, technical subjects, joint acquisition and procurement of maritime logistics, maritime training and standards, obtaining mandates from respective national governments, to matters of hydrography.

The International Maritime Organisation's (IMO) role in Africa's maritime security too has been significant. Since 2005, the IMO has sponsored a series of meetings to discuss the prospects of a regional maritime security alignment covering the wider Western Indian Ocean region. A draft regional memorandum of understanding was developed in a 2008 seminar, which became the basis of a regional agreement. The Djibouti Code of Conduct (DCoC) was signed at the follow up conference in Djibouti in January 2009.

The adoption of new forms of international regulation such as the International Ship and Port Facility Security (ISPS) Code as part of the 1974 International Convention for the Safety of Life at Sea (SOLAS) also helped to create awareness about maritime security. The ISPS code, which came into force in 2004, was the result of sustained international pressure to improve risk management at the more than 100 port facilities in Africa.

Gulf of Guinea Code of Conduct

In June 2013, heads of state and senior representatives from the Economic Community of Central African States (ECCAS) and the Economic Community of West Africa (ECOWAS) member states met in Yaoundé, Cameroon, and agreed upon a cooperative maritime strategy that focused on regional solutions to regional problems.[12] The Code of Conduct for West and Central Africa (also known as the Gulf of Guinea Code of Conduct) acknowledged the economic and geo-political importance of the maritime domain, which is critical to the continued development and future of Africa. The Gulf of Guinea Code of Conduct was initially proposed by ECOWAS and is modelled after the DCoC. This widely perceived as being the first major agreement between regional states for combating piracy in the Gulf of Guinea.[13]

AU's Maritime Security Efforts

Africa Union's interest in maritime security has grown gradually over the years. The thrust of the AU's efforts have been towards evolving a 'maritime transport charter' and a commensurate 'plan of action'. The new charter adopted at Durban in 2009, was complemented by a resolution that addressed maritime security. The so-called Durban resolution announced the agreement to cooperate, and fore grounded the importance of the ISPS code and the DCoC. It also led to the establishment of two working groups tasked to explore the possibilities of regional strategies. Work on a maritime security strategy was supposed to have started formally in April 2010.

In June 2011, a task force began work on the 2050 African Integrated Maritime (AIM) Strategy and completed it by the end of 2012. The strategy proposes a permanent review mechanism in the frame of a tri-annual revision of the strategy and an annual review of its implementation.[14] The African Union's (AU) deadline for securing the continent's territorial waters—has been set at 2050, but the target may prove elusive.

Other Security Initiatives

In 2009, the Indian Ocean Naval Symposium (IONS) came into being. Launched and initially sponsored by the Indian navy, the annual symposium includes naval representatives from the Indian Ocean littoral states and has a cross-regional format. During the third edition of the IONS conference at Cape Town in 2012, African nations led the discussions and their focus was on the potential use of high-tech sensors and communications equipment by the countries of the Indian Ocean Rim.[15]

The discussion with regard to maritime security in African waters revolved around crime, pollution and disasters on the high seas—areas where new technology was direly needed. Participants highlighted the need to identify technology that could be leveraged effectively for combating pirate attacks, and greater cooperation between the individual Maritime Search and Rescue Coordinating Centres (MRCCs) to ensure naval ships reached merchantmen in distress, expeditiously. The issues discussed, included the improvement of the Automatic Information System (AIS) and the Long Range Identification and Tracking Systems (LRIT), a satellite-based system which can track ships up to 1000 nautical miles away.[16] During the deliberation on humanitarian assistance, environmental protection and physical security measures, delegates endorsed a comprehensive system of security in all IOR nations that would ensure a secure information exchange network for the coordination of naval activity in the ever-expanding patrol zones in the Indian Ocean.

A further aspect of the maritime engagement in Africa is the setting up of the Search and Rescue (SAR) infrastructure and the Global Maritime Distress and Safety System (GMDSS). Based on the global attempt to develop the infrastructure fora monitoring and information sharing system on maritime traffic within the framework of the International Convention on Maritime Search and Rescue, a conference in 2000 decided to establish five Regional Maritime Rescue Centres (MRCCs) in Mombasa, Cape Town, Lagos, Monrovia and Morocco along with 26 Maritime Rescue Sub-Centres (MRSCs). The centres are based on multilateral treaties and are designed to work co-operatively to provide search and rescue coverage by monitoring ship movements, information sharing and coordinating rescue attempts. The first MRCC became operational in 2006 (Mombasa) and the last centre was opened in 2011 (Morocco).[17] In effect, there are presently three types of security communities trying to address the issue of maritime insecurity[18]:

(a) A continent-wide community, such as the Africa Union (AU) that has attempted to formulate an African maritime security strategy.
(b) Regional groupings, like the Southern African Development Community (SADC) and East African attempts, including activities at the Intergovernmental Authority for Development (IGAD), the Djibouti and Gulf of Guinea Code of Conduct processes.
(c) Indian Ocean communities like the IONS and IOR-ARC.

India as a 'net-security-provider' in the Western Indian Ocean

Over the past three decades, India has shown a strong commitment for providing security in its near maritime zones. It has forged an enduring security relationship with island nations in the Indian Ocean, and has even been involved (albeit modestly) in the evolving maritime security architecture of South East Asia.[19] But the Indian Ocean is India's primary zone of interest and influence. In 2012, while addressing the Naval Commanders' conference in New Delhi, Defence Minister A.K. Antony made India's security stance in the IOR clear, by stating that the "Indian navy was pursuing a string of proactive engagements with countries in the Indian Ocean region to ensure peace and stability, which is related to our economic and wider security interests."[20] India's strong security role in the IOR was confirmed by Prime Minister Manmohan Singh in 2013, when he declared that India was a "net security provider" in the Indian Ocean and stated that it was committed to "improving the maritime environment."[21]

India's engagement with the island nations in the Indian Ocean is a prime example of the Indian navy's robust involvement in maritime security in the region. India has patrolled the Mauritius EEZ since 2003, and deputes a naval officer to manage the National Coast Guard of Mauritius. India laid the foundation of its naval security cooperation with Mauritius with the gift of a seaward defence boat—the *INS Amar* in 1974.[22] Since then, it has been periodically providing Mauritius with maritime reconnaissance assets—including an interceptor patrol boat (2001), three Dornier Do 228 maritime surveillance aircraft (in 2004 and 2010),[23] a Dhruv helicopter (2009), and three new Islander aircraft engines (2013). The *CGS Barracuda*—a new offshore patrol vessel being built by the GRSE, Kolkata—is due for delivery in 2014.[24] India has also helped Mauritius in installing an Automated Identification System (AIS) and a Coastal Surveillance Radar System.

In addition to providing maritime assets and training, the Indian navy also carries out hydrographic surveys, and assists the Mauritian Coast Guard ships in EEZ surveillance and joint patrols. During a visit to Mauritius in February, 2013, the Indian navy chief Admiral D.K. Joshi handed over an inshore hydrographic survey vessel to Mauritius on New

Delhi's behalf. India also recently announced it would deliver a new offshore patrol vessel to Mauritius in 2014, for use in anti-piracy operations, and for fight illegal fishing and drug trafficking.[25]

The Indian navy and coast guard also assist Seychelles in maintaining security by undertaking maritime surveillance, hydrographic surveys, and providing training, and maritime military equipment and repair. In 2005, India gave the Seychelles Coast Guard a fast-attack vessel the, *INS Tarmugli*, one Do-228 aircraft and two Chetak helicopters in 2010. In the last few years, the navy has been deploying Dorniers and helicopters in Seychelles on a regular basis as well as stepping up the visits of its warships to the region to help in anti-piracy operation. The latest Indian aircraft to be handed over to Seychelles was a Do-228 in Feb 2013.[26]

Beyond bilateral relationships, New Delhi's strong leadership role in Indian Ocean institutions, such as the Indian Ocean Rim-Association for Regional Cooperation (IOR-ARC) and the Indian Ocean Naval Symposium (IONS) reinforces its strong security relationships with Island states in the Western Indian Ocean Region.

India's Military Diplomacy in Africa

As a part of its defence diplomacy, India has invested in the training of officers from a number of African countries in its defence academies and service colleges. Among the beneficiaries was Nigeria's Olusegun Obasanjo (President: 1999-2007). He initiated moves to strengthening defence cooperation with India. As a result, India was involved in the transformation of the Nigerian Defence Academy in Kaduna into a degree-granting military university.

In 2007, the possibility of including a naval component within the IBSA alliance was explored for the first time during a meeting between Vice Admiral Mudimo, chief of the naval staff of the South African navy and his Indian counterpart, Admiral Sureesh Mehta, where they discussed the creation of a mechanism for cooperation to deal with terrorism and piracy.[27] It led to the formalisation of the IBSA joint naval exercises (IBSAMAR). Since 2008, three editions of the exercises have been held off the South African coast with the aim of establishing common tactical approaches and procedural interoperability of forces.

As mentioned earlier, the Indian navy has been extending its maritime security cover to most of the islands of the Western Indian Ocean. Since 2003, when a bilateral accord was signed between India and Mauritius, the IN has patrolled the latter's EEZ. A similar deal led to patrols off the territorial waters of Seychelles. In June/July 2003 a destroyer and a frigate (*INS Ranjit, INS Suvarna*) were deployed off Maputo to provide security for the Africa summit taking place there. In June of the following year two OPV's (*INS Sujata, INS Savitri*) assisted in providing security to the world economic forum in Mozambique. This led to the eventual signing of a MoU in 2006, whereby India agreed to mount regular maritime patrols off the Mozambique coast.

In 2007, India established a radar surveillance station with a sophisticated digital system to track shipping in the Western Indian Ocean. There have been rumours of India's interest in leasing the remote Agalega islands from Mauritius, possibly for a naval base. The Indian defence industrial complex has made some forays into Africa by supplying seaward defence boats and light helicopters. India is also a customer of South Africa's arms exports industry.[28] India's endeavours indicate a new appreciation of maritime outreach in Africa. Defence agreements have therefore been signed with Kenya, Madagascar, and Mozambique, and joint training exercises undertaken with Kenya, Mozambique, Tanzania, and South Africa. India's 2007 memorandum of understanding (MoU) with Mozambique envisaged the maritime patrolling of the waters off the latter's coast, supplying military equipment, training personnel, and transferring technical know-how in assembling and repairing military vehicles, aircraft and ships. This seems to be the template India would like to follow with other partners in Africa.

China's Maritime Aid to Africa

As it looks to enhance its maritime engagement, India has also been keeping a wary eye on China's expanding security footprint in Africa. Beijing's emergence as the leading source of military aid to Africa, has not escaped New Delhi's attention. An example of China's creeping security footprint is Nigeria—a major source of energy for Beijing. After an unsuccessful bid to enlist U.S. help for fighting Islamist insurgent in its oil-rich Niger Delta, Nigeria turned to China for arms, equipment, training and technology for the Nigerian armed forces.[29] With the result that the People's Liberation Army now imparts training and provides arms, which include Chinese-made supersonic F-7 fighter aircraft. China is helping Nigeria develop a squadron of F-7s, which will form the backbone of the Nigerian Air Force.[30]

Other African countries too are becoming increasingly dependent on Chinese military aid. In early 2013, Ghana commissioned four new Chinese patrol boats, and Namibia acquired a 100m refurbished Chinese patrol vessel, adding to a naval complement that includes harbour and inshore patrol boats. There is also a growing trend towards aerial reconnaissance over the ocean, especially in West Africa, with Ghana and Nigeria acquiring aircraft for monitoring and addressing piracy.

China's efforts to expand its footprint in Seychelles and Mauritius are also significant. In 2011, there were reports that Seychelles had offered China a base for its ships deployed in the Gulf of Aden and the Western Indian Ocean to combat piracy in that region.[31] While there were no indications that the offer had been accepted, Chinese media reported that China was actively considering using it as a' resupply' base. This prompted China's foreign ministry to clarify that China was not contemplating a military base in Seychelles because it would 'violate' its policy of' not stationing troops abroad.[32] Interestingly, China did not deny that such an offer had indeed been made by Seychelles.

Similarly, Chinese President Hu Jintao announced many economic packages during his visit to Mauritius in February 2009. These included a grant of$260 million to expand the island nation's airport. Between the recognition of China by Mauritius in 1972 and Hu's visit in February 2009, the total value of the Chinese assistance to Mauritius amounted to $117 million.[33] The fresh assistance extended since then has crossed the one billion dollar mark—an almost ten-fold increase.[34] India's concerns over Beijing's deepening ties with Seychelles and Mauritius are that these are the countries that had historically looked to India as their main defence provider.

Improving India-Africa Maritime Cooperation

While India must start by cooperating with African countries on basic maritime security issues such as improving maritime domain awareness, building local policing ability, and training of personnel, it will eventually need to provide assistance for the development of an African maritime economy and a comprehensive strategy for maritime development. As Africa looks to enlist the support of regional and international partners for help to integrate existing institutions and projects into a self-sustaining maritime system, India will need to step forward. In operational terms, this will mean greater assistance in local capacity building, training of personnel, professional guidance in specific maritime functions, legal infrastructure support, and assistance for hydrographic surveys and coast guard duties.

India's near-term plan must be to provide resources, assets and technology to African navies and coast guards to help them perform basic constabulary functions. In the long-term, India must assist in the creation of an African maritime system that enables the optimum utilisation of Africa's resources. In practical terms, this translates into assistance for capacity building, infrastructure creation, law enforcement and good governance.

Through a collaborative arrangement, India could assist in the creation of an African maritime sector that generates the security, confidence, and efficiency necessary to kick-start investment, trade, and create jobs vital for the continent's prosperity. By collectively revolutionising the African maritime sector, and revitalising the maritime economy, India and Africa will have an opportunity to jointly forge a truly robust maritime partnership.

NOTES

1. "India now Nigeria's biggest crude oil buyer", *The Hindu*, July 15, 2013, http://www.thehindu.com /business/Industry/india-now-nigerias-biggest-crude-oil-buyer/article4917091.ece (Accessed on November 11, 2013)
2. "Tackling predators: Anti-piracy operations in Gulf of Aden", *Centre for Asian Studies – India*, Mar 2010, http://www.cassindia.com/inner_page.php?id=21&&task=terrorism (Accessed on November 11, 2013)
3. "Roles and Expectations of Emerging Navies in Cooperative Engagement for Peace and Stability in IOR", Operational Seminar and Preparatory Workshop for IONS – 2013, Keynote address by Dr C Raja Mohan, at http://ions.gov.in/sites/default/files/BriefonIONSSem_PrepWork_Sep_2013_0.pdf. (Accessed November 11, 2013).
4. Christian Bueger, "Communities of Security Practice at Work -A Review of Maritime Security Cooperation in Africa, *African Security*, Special Issue, 2013.

5. Michael L. Baker, "Towards an African Maritime Economy - Empowering the African Union to Revolutionize the African Maritime Sector, *Naval War College Review,* Spring 2011, 64(2), p 39.
6. Bueger, p. 8.
7. Paul Musili Wambua, "Enhancing regional maritime cooperation in Africa: the planned end state", *African Security Review*, Institute of Security Studies, 2009, p 48-49
8. Ibid, p. 9.
9. "South Africa as an Anti-Piracy Actor", *e-International Relations*, Nov 6, 2012, http://www.e-ir.info/2012/11/06/anti-piracy-actors-south-africa/ (Accessed on November 15, 2013)
10. "Terms of reference—Drafting of a Somalia Inland Action Plan to counter and prevent Piracy 2010-2015", IGAD Secretariat, July 21, 2010
11. Frank Van Rooyen, "Africa and the Geo-politics of the Indian Ocean", *Occasional paper 78*, South Africa Institute of International Affairs, available at www.saiia.org.za/doc.../67-africa-and-the-geopolitics-of-the-indian-ocean (Accessed on Nov. 12, 2013).
12. Captain (Ret.) Phillip J. Heyl, "West and Central African Leaders Unite Against Piracy in the Gulf of Guinea", Paper presented during the 3rd *UAE Counter Piracy Conference*, Sept 11, 2013, available at http://www.counterpiracy.ae/upload/2013briefing/Heyl%20Phil-Sec1Ch6-%20Final%20Briefing%20Paper-En-Website.pdf (Accessed on Nov 11, 2013)
13. Ibid, p 2.
14. "Task Force to Lead Development and Implementation of 2050 Africa's Integrated Maritime Strategy Formed", *Africa Union Press Release* No. 064/2011, available at http://au.int/en/content/task-force-lead-development-and-implementation-2050-africa%E2%80%99s-integrated-maritime-strategy-20 (Accessed on November 11, 2013)
15. Abhijit Singh, "IONS At Cape Town", *National Maritime Foundation* Commentary, Apr 2012, maritimeindia.org/article/ions-cape-town-towards-greater-maritime-security (Accessed on November 11, 2013).
16. Ibid.
17. Bueger, p. 11.
18. Bueger, p. 8.
19. The Indian navy has been sending its ships regularly to South East Asia and has been taking part in the ADMM plus exercises. India is also a member of the Expanded ASEAN Maritime Forum (EAMF)
20. Antony Envisages a Proactive Role for Navy in the Indian Ocean Region, Press release Ministry of Defence, Oct 18, 2012, http://pib.nic.in/newsite/erelease.aspx?relid=88491 (Accessed on November 6, 2013)
21. "India well positioned to become a net provider of security: Manmohan Singh", *The Hindu*, May 4, 2013, http://www.thehindu.com/news/national/india-well-positioned-to-become-a-net-provider-of-security-manmohan-singh/article4742337.ece (Accessed on November 11, 2013)
22. "Transfer Of Naval Ships To Foreign Navies", The Indian navy's official website http://indiannavy.nic.in/print/book/export/html/992, also see Sudha Ramachandran, "India's quiet sea power", *Asia Times,* Aug. 2, 2007, available at http://www.atimes.com/atimes/South_Asia/ IH02Df01.html (Accessed on November 12, 2013)
23. "India donates Do 228 surveillance aircraft to Seychelles", *Defence Web*, Feb 4, 2013, http://www.defenceweb.co.za/index.php?option=com_content&view=article&id=29310&catid=74&Itemid=30 (Accessed on November 13, 2013)
24. "Mauritius to receive Indian-built patrol vessel", *Defence Web*, Aug 19, 2013, http://

www.defenceweb.co.za/index.php?option=com_content&view=article&id=31585:mauritius-to-receive-indian-built-patrol-vessel&catid=51:Sea&Itemid=106 (Accessed on November 10, 2013)

25. "Mauritius to receive Indian-built patrol vessel", *Defence Web*, Aug 19, 2013, http://www.defenceweb.co.za/index.php?option=com_content&view=article&id=31585:mauritius-to-receive-indian-built-patrol-vessel&catid=51:Sea&Itemid=106 (Accessed on November 12, 2013).
26. "India presents Donier Aircraft to Seyclelles, *Times of India,* Feb 1, 2013, available at http://articles.timesofindia.indiatimes.com/2013-02-01/india/36683369_1_dornier-228-maritime-reconnaissance-aircraft-seychelles (Accessed on November 11, 2013)
27. Vijay Sakhuja, " IBSA Navies: Strengthening Maritime Multilateralism", *South Asia Defence and Strategic Review*, available at http://www.defstrat.com/exec/frmArticleDetails.aspx?DID=191 (Accessed on November 12, 2013).
28. Peter Pham, "India in Africa: Implications of an Emerging Power for AFRICOM and US Strategy" *SSA Monograph.* March 2011
29. Joseph Fareh, "China Africa Influence Expanding", available at http://www.wnd.com/2012/08 /chinas-african-influence-expanding/ (Accessed on November 10, 2012)
30. Ibid.
31. K.K. Agnihotri, "Chinese Quest for a Naval Base in The Indian Ocean", *National Maritime Foundation Commentary*, Feb 2010, http://www.maritimeindia.org/article/chinese-quest-naval-base-indian-ocean-%E2%80%93-possible-options-china.html (Accessed on November 12, 2013)
32. Mandip Singh, "The Proposed PLA Naval Base in Seychelles and India's Options", *IDSA Comment*, December 15, 2011 at http://www.idsa.in/idsacomments/TheProposedPLANavalBaseinSeychellesand IndiasOptions_msingh_15121 (Accessed on November 11, 2013)
33. Amit Kumar, "China's Island Strategy in the Indian Ocean: Breaching India's Sphere of Influence", *ORF Issue Brief*,http://www.observerindia.com/cms/sites/orfonline /modules/analysis/attachments /influence_1253251335478.pdf (Accessed on November 10, 2013)
34. B. Raman, "India and the Indian Ocean", *Global Geo-politics and Political Economy*, Nov 2011, http://globalgeopolitics.net/wordpress/2011/02/28/india-the-indian-ocean/ (Accessed on November 12, 2013)

9

Energy Challenges Facing India and Africa: Building a Sustainable Partnership

Shebonti Ray Dadwal

Introduction

The Global Energy Scenario

The current price of crude oil is ruling at prices that are 50 per cent lower than they were less than a year ago, and although this has presented energy importing countries with an opportunity to cut their energy import bills, and given some much needed relief to their economies, this can only be a temporary reprieve. Given the political nature of the oil industry, economics has less to do with the current pricing than geopolitical considerations. Nevertheless, it is only a matter of time before oil, and other energy prices rebound as demand increases because of low prices, and because of companies raising the huge sums of money required for increasing production. Given the long time lag before a field can be brought into production, it is highly probable that before long oil prices will rise sharply, before going south once again.

Even in the case of natural gas, the price has come down sharply, due to the advent of shale gas following the 'fracking' (hydraulic fracturing) revolution in the US since 2007-08. But as the gas market is regional, rather than global, large importers of non-American gas have not seen any substantial price cuts. Even American energy buyers may soon have to pay higher prices, as the production of shale gas has been impacted by low oil prices as well as excess supplies as the steep fall in prices has made it difficult to keep production going and has impacted investment.

Therefore, in the long term, for countries seeking a modicum of self-sufficiency, or at least looking to keep their soaring fossil fuel import bills under control, renewable energy resources are the best option. According to the *International Energy Outlook Report* of the US Energy Information Administration (EIA), "In many parts of the world, concerns about security of energy supplies and the environmental consequences of greenhouse gas emissions have spurred government policies that support a projected increase in renewable energy sources."[1]

It is in this context that the energy security challenges of emerging economies like India and most African countries need to be analysed.

India's Energy Challenge

India's energy challenge is best highlighted by the following excerpt from the *Integrated Energy Policy*, published by the Planning Commission in 2006.

> India faces formidable challenges in meeting its energy needs and in providing adequate energy of desired quality in various forms in a sustainable manner and at competitive prices. India needs to sustain an 8% to 10% economic growth rate, over the next 25 years, if it is to eradicate poverty and meet its human development goals. To deliver a sustained growth rate of 8% through 2031-32 and to meet the lifeline energy needs of all citizens, India needs, at the very least, to increase its primary energy supply by 3 to 4 times and, its electricity generation capacity/supply by 5 to 6 times of their 2003-04 levels. With 2003-04 as the base, India's commercial energy supply would need to grow from 5.2% to 6.1% per annum while its total primary energy supply would need to grow at 4.3% to 5.1% annually.

India is currently the fourth-largest energy consumer in the world, with a consumption (in 2012) of 563 million tonnes of oil equivalent (mtoe), as compared to China's 2,735 mtoe, the US' 2,209 mtoe and Russia's 694 mtoe. Moreover, India's per capita consumption of energy is about 456 kilogramme of oil equivalent (kgoe) which is less than a third of the global average. As a result, India's energy consumption is expected to increase exponentially across the board.

The nature of the challenge can be gauged from the fact that despite a high installed capacity of 2,25,000 MW, around 40 per cent of the population has little or no access to electricity, and is largely dependent on biomass, which in turn contributes to carbon emissions and exacerbates India's climate change challenges. The second challenge for India is that, like its counterparts in the developing world, it is highly dependent on fossil fuels, and will continue to remain so in the foreseeable future. However, India's hydrocarbon resources are limited, and its dependence on oil, gas and coal imports is increasing year-on-year. India's dependence on energy imports has seen a huge outgo of foreign exchange—$144 billion in the last fiscal—and is the largest part of its overall import bill. Hence, in order to reduce this dependency, India has been trying to augment its renewable and nuclear energy baskets.

In the case of nuclear energy, while the target has been set at around 63,000 MW by 2032, India's inadequate reserves of uranium necessitate imports of the same. Given its compulsion to meet its development and poverty eradication goals, India's requirement for coal, which is the bedrock of the power sector will increase. As a result, despite having large reserves of coal, India's coal imports have gone up by almost a quarter of its total demand. In order to reduce its dependence on coal, as well as to lower carbon emissions, India has been looking to substitute coal with gas-based power generation. As a result, India's gas (LNG) imports have also seen a steady rise since 2005. According to some statistics, India's dependence on imported natural gas is expected to increase from 26 per cent in 2012 to 54 per cent in 2021-2022.

The transport sector, which is overwhelmingly dependent on oil, is expected to almost double from 10 per cent in 2010, to 20 per cent in 2040, in terms of total energy consumption. As a result, despite the reduction in the use of oil in the power sector, oil imports have risen to comprise almost 80 per cent of overall demand. Given that India's oil production has not seen any growth over the last several years, the country's import dependency is expected to rise to around 90 per cent by 2020.

With regard to the power sector, despite having the fifth largest installed generation capacity in the world of around 258 GW, over 40 per cent of rural and six per cent of urban households in India do not have access to modern forms of energy. Unless addressed urgently, this shortfall will increase manifold, as by 2028, India is expected to overtake China as the world's most populated country, with 1.45 billion people. According to statistics, the primary energy demand in 2010 stood at 691 million tonnes of oil equivalent (mtoe). Of this, about 41 per cent comprised of coal; 24 per cent liquid (mainly oil, 23 per cent non-commercial fuel); 8 per cent gas, with the remainder a mix of hydro, renewables and nuclear power. Hence, despite years of trying to develop alternative energy resources, including renewable energy and nuclear power, India remains a predominantly fossil fuel-based economy.[2] Moreover, according to statistics put out by different government organisations and policy papers, the total installed generation capacity by 2031 will be required to be between 778 GW (as per the Integrated Energy Policy of 2006), and 962 GW (as per the Ministry of Power).

India's energy infrastructure is based on a centralised model of power generation, transmission and distribution which, as demand grows exponentially, is becoming increasingly costly to maintain. At the same time, given the current dependence on fossil fuels, the increasing dependence on imports, would translate into a huge outgo of foreign exchange, putting the country's economy in dire straits. Therefore, India needs to encourage a decentralised business model in order to more readily take advantage of the abundantly available renewable energy sources, like solar, wind, hydropower, biomass, biogas, geothermal and hydrogen energy, and fuel cells.

The current NDA government has taken the decision to promote renewable energy, and focus on solar, wind, geothermal and conventional hydropower to meet future energy demand. As a result, the government has revised the renewable based power generation capacity addition to 100 GW in solar by 2022, from the current capacity of 3 GW; and 60 GW in wind based power, from the current capacity of 21 GW. Moreover, the government is also trying to do away with the subsidy regime in the sector, and is devising ways of trying to incentivise investors in renewable energy projects. One of the options being looked at is the inclusion of a 'renewable purchase obligation' (RPO) in the Electricity Act-2014. But given that the current installed capacity of renewables from all sources is about 31 GW (31,692.14 MW) only, that is, 12 per cent of total capacity, while actual generation is less than 6 per cent, can renewable energy ramp up generation to meet the growing demand?

According to a report in *Clean Technica*, India is blessed with 300-330 sunny days a year, and can easily generate 5000 trillion kWh of solar energy, which is higher than India's total annual energy consumption. Using the country's deserts and farm land, India could easily install around 1,000 GW of solar generation capacity– equivalent to around four times the current peak power generation. Moreover, with wind energy generation along its 7,500 km of coastline, India can generate up to 170 GW. Hydropower can produce an estimated 148 GW, geothermal around 10.7 GW and tidal power about 15 GW, according to a report of the environmental group World Wide Fund for Nature.[3]

All renewable energy power projects can be set up at a fast pace as against conventional power projects which take up to five to six years to get started. Moreover, unlike fossil fuel-based projects that have to be sourced often from great distances, renewable energy projects can be built from materials that are locally available and have a virtually limitless supply. While they can be installed as stand-alone, off-grid projects, thereby allowing each village to have its own power station, they can also be connected to the grid systems of the state-owned or other utilities wherever feasible. Furthermore, the renewable route also offers job opportunities to local people, as the task of operating, and maintaining these facilities, can be effectively handled by locally trained personnel.

Finally, and most importantly, renewable energy is becoming increasingly feasible from a financial perspective, which removes the biggest hurdle to widespread use. The initial cost of installation is becoming increasingly more competitive vis-à-vis conventional energy. Hence, a solar device that cost more than \$2 per watt a few years ago, is now available for 50 cents a watt. However, it is important that a policy framework is put in place at the earliest.[4]

To enhance its energy security by reducing dependence on hydrocarbon imports, India embarked on a programme to develop its vast renewable energy potential, and today has an impressive installed capacity of around 29,464.51 MW, that includes hydro, wind and biogas and solar energy. Moreover, the government has launched an ambitious national solar energy programme under the National Action Plan on Climate Change, for generating some 20,000 MW of solar power by 2021-22, along with a biofuel programme to further rein in its increasing dependence on oil imports.

Nevertheless, given the volume of demand, India does not have the luxury of being selective in its energy choices, but has to explore and exploit all energy resource options.

More importantly, India will remain dependent on hydrocarbons for the foreseeable future, and this is where African countries assume importance as energy sources and partners. With 9 per cent of oil reserves that constitute around 13 per cent of the world's oil production; 7.9 per cent of the world's natural gas reserves; 5 per cent of coal reserves (of which, South Africa with 3.7 per cent, provides the bulk); and 38 per cent of uranium reserves, Africa is increasingly being seen as an important energy source. Interestingly, over the next 10-15 years, according to forecasts, most of the new oil entering the world market will be coming from Africa.

There are other reasons why Africa has become a favoured destination for energy seekers. While technological advances have allowed Africa's deep offshore resources to become accessible, African crude comprises mostly of low-sulphur and light to medium gravity, which makes it attractive to refiners. Moreover, Africa, particularly the west coast, is conveniently situated geographically to serve both North American and European markets.

This positional advantage is further enhanced by the fact that many recent finds are offshore which in turn reduces the security, health and infrastructure problems that could be associated with onshore work. Furthermore, floating production and storage facilities support oil companies' efforts offshore as they can produce the oil, store it and then transport it all close to the well offshore. Approximately 64 per cent of

India's imported oil came from West Asian countries in 2012. The second biggest source of imports is Africa (17 per cent), with the majority of the oil coming from Nigeria.

Africa's Energy Challenge

Despite the fact that Africa has emerged as an important global source for hydrocarbons, most countries in the continent are energy-poor, including the oil and gas rich countries in North and West Africa. For example, Nigeria, which is the largest producer of oil in the continent, is unable to generate even 4000 MW of electricity.[5] According to the estimates of the International Finance Corporation (IFC) of the 600 million people in Africa, around 70 per cent did not have access to electricity as of September 2012. More specifically, according to the International Energy Agency (IEA), sub-Saharan Africa has the lowest percentage of access to electricity, ranging from 24 to 32 per cent with rural electricity access averaging a dismal 8 per cent; while the Eastern Africa sub-region poses the most significant challenge to the global energy access issue.

Over the last few years, the situation has deteriorated further due to the global economic recession and the lack of investment. Only 10 per cent of the infrastructure investments in the region went toward energy as compared to 44 per cent in South Asia; 39 per cent in East Asia and the Pacific; 35 per cent in Latin America; and 22 per cent in the Middle East-North Africa (MENA) region. On the other hand, the demand for electricity has grown exponentially, making it one of the highest energy consuming regions in the world.

Moreover, most of the African countries lack the technology, human resource skills, infrastructure, and the regulatory and governance mechanisms that are needed to convert their natural resources into modern and usable forms of energy. At the same time, given that most African countries have a low installed power capacity, and are currently on a growth trajectory, they are on course to selecting a more sustainable energy path that is different from the Western fossil fuel dependent model. Moreover, like India, most African countries are blessed with abundant renewable energy resources, like solar and wind. It is in this respect that India, as a development partner, can provide assistance to African governments, as India has gone through similar experiences in its developmental path.

Roadmap for a more Sustainable Energy Partnership

Although Indian companies are active in the hydrocarbon E&P sectors of African countries, New Delhi has been charged with taking a mercantilist approach similar to that adopted by other countries. India has however reiterated that its Africa policy is based on a model that combines resource extraction with long-term development in the host country or region. According to J. Peter Pham, a senior fellow and director of the Africa Project at the New York-based National Committee on American Foreign Policy, India has adopted a policy of adding value to its investments and is attempting to integrate itself into the economy, rather than simply viewing the country as "a supply depot for resources"—the rationale being that aiding African development, leads to a more conducive and sustainable relationship between the two regions. He terms this a "hybrid model", a cross between the Western model, which largely depends on private investment in Africa, and the Chinese and Russian models, that are state-driven.[6]

This would of course entail Indian entrepreneurs to increase their investments in the African energy infrastructure sector, as well as expand and develop a pool of local expertise, rather than adopt a mercantilist policy as some countries have tended to do. Indian companies should take initiatives that would promote green technologies, develop local expertise for Africa's rural electrification process—both on and off grid—and promote projects in partnership with African companies for production of alternative sources of energy. Moreover, many African countries do not have large hydrocarbon resources, and even those that do require more sustainable and cleaner forms of energy to combat climate change pressures.

India is well placed to provide assistance to African governments in their quest for sustainable development. Being the first and only country with a dedicated Ministry of New and Renewable Energy (MNRE), India is well suited to provide assistance in this area to African countries. India has had long experience in developing indigenous, non-traditional energy resources—solar, wind and biogas—which in turn has seen the share of renewable energy increase to around 10 per cent of overall generation capacity. Indian wind turbine manufacturers are among the world's leading companies in this sector. India is currently in the process of reviewing its biofuel programme—which can be emulated by the African countries.

Most of the African states are well equipped to exploit the huge potential in renewable energy resources, particularly solar energy given that the continent receives an average of 6kW/h of solar energy per square metre every day. Moreover, with rising concerns relating to climate change, Africa will find itself coming under increasing pressure to find low-carbon alternatives to replace traditional fuels. The adoption of renewable energy in Africa will be a huge opportunity to improve socio-economic indices and living standards. Better access to electricity will also go a long way in alleviating poverty and ensuring environmental sustainability. In many parts of Africa, millions live far away from developed towns and cities and are not connected to the grid.

That African leaders realise the potential for renewable energy and indeed the importance of developing capacity in this sector to address their long-term energy demand for energy, is clear from the number of renewable energy conferences held in various parts of the continent. In fact several initiatives such as the African Renewable Energy Network on Combating Desertification and Green Wall for the Sahara Initiative have been taken, with a view to addressing climate change issues as well as seeking alternatives to hydrocarbons.

As developing countries and a shared history of colonial exploitation, India and Africa face common energy security challenges. While India is a large and growing market for energy, many African countries have large hydrocarbon resources which can be exploited for financing their economies, while others have large untapped potential for renewable energy that can be harnessed to resolve their energy poverty. Indian companies have over the years gained expertise in the energy sector, and can provide assistance in the same. As Togo's Prime Minister Gilbert Fossoun Houngbo said in 2010, "What is very interesting and appealing is the Indian model of cooperation. India is a developing country but has achieved much. Africa can, therefore, learn from the trajectory of development in India and the Indian experience."[7]

NOTES

1. http://www.eia.gov/forecasts/ieo/more_highlights.cfm (Accessed February 9, 2015).
2. Vipul Tuli, Amit Khera, India: Towards Energy Independence 2030", McKinsey & Co., January 2014, file:///C:/Users/shebonti/Downloads/India_Towards_energy_independence_2030.pdf (Accessed February 10, 2015).

3. Darshan Goswami, Can India Achieve 100% Renewable Energy? *CleanTechnica*, August 21, 2014, http://cleantechnica.com/2014/08/21/can-india-achieve-100-renewable-energy-future/ (Accessed September 21, 2014).
4. Manu Rishi Puri, Empowering rural India via the renewable route, *Business Today*, February 9, 2015, http://businesstoday.intoday.in/story/empowering-rural-india-via-the-renewable-route/1/215531.html (Accessed February 10, 2015).
5. Kingsley Ighobar, "There is energy momentum in Africa", *Africa Renewal*, April 2014, http://www.un.org/africarenewal/magazine/april-2014/there-energy-momentum-africa (Accessed September 22, 2015.
6. Fawzia Sheikh, "India Facing Fierce Competition in its Search for Oil and Natural Gas Resources," Oilprice.com, December 24, 2009, http://oilprice.com/Geo-Politics/ASia/India-FAcing-Fierce-Competition-in-its-Search-for-Oil-and-Natural-Gas-Resources.html (Accessed September 12, 2014).
7. Manish Chand, Comparing India with China in Africa", *Africa Quarterly*, 50(1), February-April 2010, http://indiaafricaquarterly.in/africa%20quarterly/Feb-April-201.pdf (Accessed September 12, 2014).

10

India's Energy Security Issues and African Oil

Aparajita Biswas

Introduction

The energy security issue has assumed colossal importance in India, mainly because energy consumption, following the trajectory of economic growth, has increased tremendously. According to the projections made by the World Energy Outlook, India's energy needs are likely to balloon over the coming decades and will be driven by its quest to maintain the high levels of economic growth (around 6-7 percent annually) that it has achieved since 1994. Recent data indicates that domestic production of crude oil actually accounts for only a quarter of India's energy demand, or even less. It has been reported that India is the world's fifth largest consumer of energy, and by 2030 it is expected to become the third largest, overtaking Japan and Russia. India's crude oil demand in 2016-17 is estimated at 186.2 million metric tonnes, according to a petroleum ministry working group report.

Coupled with this, research undertaken by Mumbai's Strategic Foresight Group predicts that by 2030, 90 percent of India's oil and gas will have to be imported... and its dependence on imported oil, which is already greater (in terms of percentage of oil consumed) than that of USA and China, is expected to increase even further. The most disquieting point is that as a result of the growing demand India imports 60 percent of its oil, worth about $21 billion a year, from West Asia, which constitutes four percent of its Gross Domestic Product (GDP).

Furthermore, there has also been a remarkable increase in the consumption of natural gas from 0.7 BCM in 1970-71 to 51.3 BCM in 2010-11, with a CAGR of 11.25 percent over the period. The industry wise off take of natural gas shows that natural gas has been used both for energy (69 percent) and non-energy (31 percent) purposes and the maximum use of natural gas is in power generation (46 percent) followed by the fertiliser industry.

Surprisingly, although India has been faced with a huge deficit and critical crisis in its oil sector for many years, it did not have energy security policy. There is a growing recognition that energy security needs to be a critical component of India's foreign and energy policy. Energy security has been defined by India's political leadership as being able to "supply lifeline energy to all our citizens as well as meet their effective demand for safe and convenient energy at affordable cost." This has been voiced time and again by India's senior political leadership[1].

It was only, in August 2006, that an Integrated Energy Policy report on enhancing India's energy security in a holistic and sustainable manner was published. Energy is now perceived as being critical for fulfilling India's development agenda. The Integrated Energy Policy recognised that an adequate supply of oil (and other hydrocarbons) is essential for India's planned economic growth of 8-10 percent over the next three decades. The plan envisioned a two-prong strategy. One track would accelerate efforts to find and produce oil at home. The other would empower Indian companies to find equity oil abroad.

The objectives of its external policy and oil security are three: (i) Putting in place a comprehensive policy that will include the total deregulation of overseas E&P businesses and empowering them to compete with international oil companies by provision of fiscal and tax benefits; (ii) Evolving a mechanism to leverage India's "Buyer Power" to obtain quality E&P projects abroad; (iii) Having a focused approach towards E&P

projects and build strong relations in focus countries with high attractiveness like Russia, Iraq, Iran and countries in North Africa.

The government of India has not only de-regulated the market-driven oil and gas industry, it has also empowered the PSU oil companies to acquire stakes in foreign oilfields. Increasingly, large private-sector companies—especially those with strong political leverage, as for example Reliance, Tata and Essar—are playing a greater role in defining the domestic energy agenda; but these companies are also proving critical for putting together the components, both financial and political, that are necessary for successful international projects[2].

The Indian government supported the Oil & Natural Gas Corporation (ONGC) of India and its export arm, the ONGC Videsh Limited (OVL), in making overseas investments and acquisitions in various oil-rich countries. The ONGC has been encouraged to seek income and rent from the upstream sector i.e. exploration and production. The urgency for such an external push was prompted by the high energy and commodity prices. Thereafter, the OVL was created with the mission to pursue 'equity oil' investments. It became very active in Africa, since the continent is richly endowed with energy, minerals and other key resources. Figure 1 illustrates this point.

Figure 1: OLV's in Africa

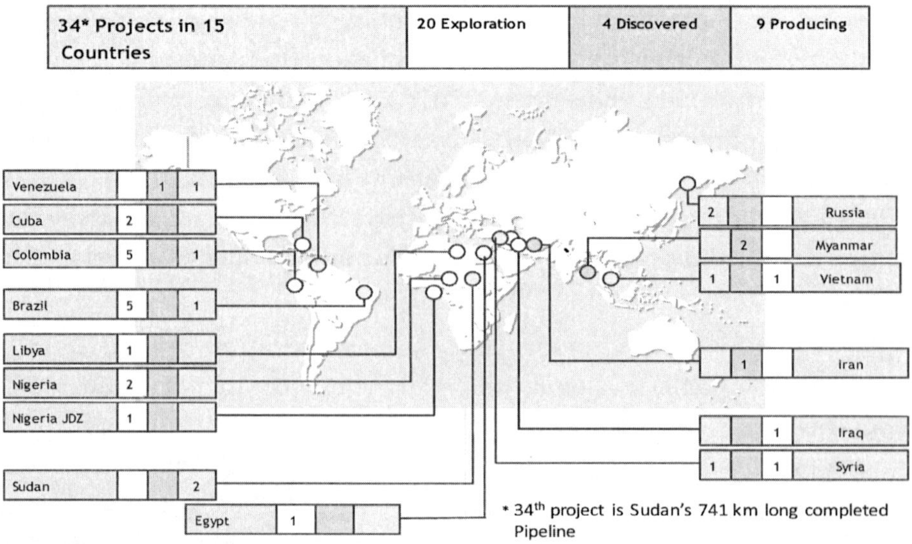

Source: ONGC.

In the light of its energy needs, India is looking for new and diversified oil sources. Africa is an extremely attractive option. African oil is of high quality, and, with the many new discoveries outside conflict zones, the continent is open for foreign participation. Only Nigeria is a member of OPEC, which sets limits on member countries' output levels. In fact the discovery of vast energy sources has enhanced the strategic importance of the continent. This paper explores Africa's oil scenario and also details the measures India has taken to engage oil rich African countries in order to meet its oil needs. An over view of Africa's growing oil sector is as follows:

Africa's Oil Scenario

Africa is in the midst of an oil and gas boom that is attracting major external interests and financial investments. It has emerged as an important player in the global oil and gas industry. Some analysts believe that the African continent has now become a vital arena of strategic and geopolitical competition between old and new powers because it is one of the most promising regions of the world for future oil production[3].

The factor responsible for the growing importance of African energy supplies is that most the countries are trying to reduce their oil dependence on West Asian countries, because of volatile situations and instability.

According to figures from the US EIA, Africa's proven oil reserves have risen significantly by nearly 120 per cent over the past three decades, from 57 billion barrels in 1980 to 124 billion barrels in 2012, with more waiting to be discovered offshore. In addition to this, Africa's proven reserves of natural gas have grown from 210 trillion cubic feet (tcf) in 1980 to 509 tcf in 2012, representing an increase of over 140 per cent. Furthermore, recent discoveries of sizable natural gas reserves in Tanzania and Mozambique point to the significant upward potential for these figures.

North African countries like Libya, Algeria and Egypt, have been substantial producers of hydrocarbons in the African continent for a number of years, with Libya having the continent's largest reserves of oil. Besides, there are also some smaller oil producing states in the north, including Tunisia, Morocco and Mauritania. In recent years sub-Saharan African countries are also producing significant quantities of oil.

Figure 2: Africa's Proven Reserves of Crude Oil (billion barrels)

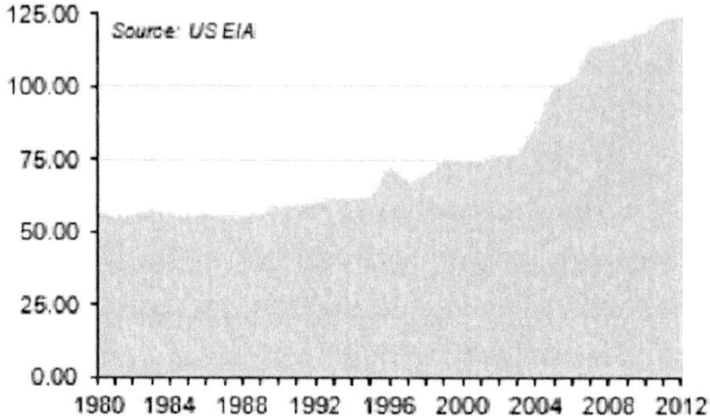

Source: Energy Insight.

Figure 3: Oil Production in Africa since 1965 predicted to 2015

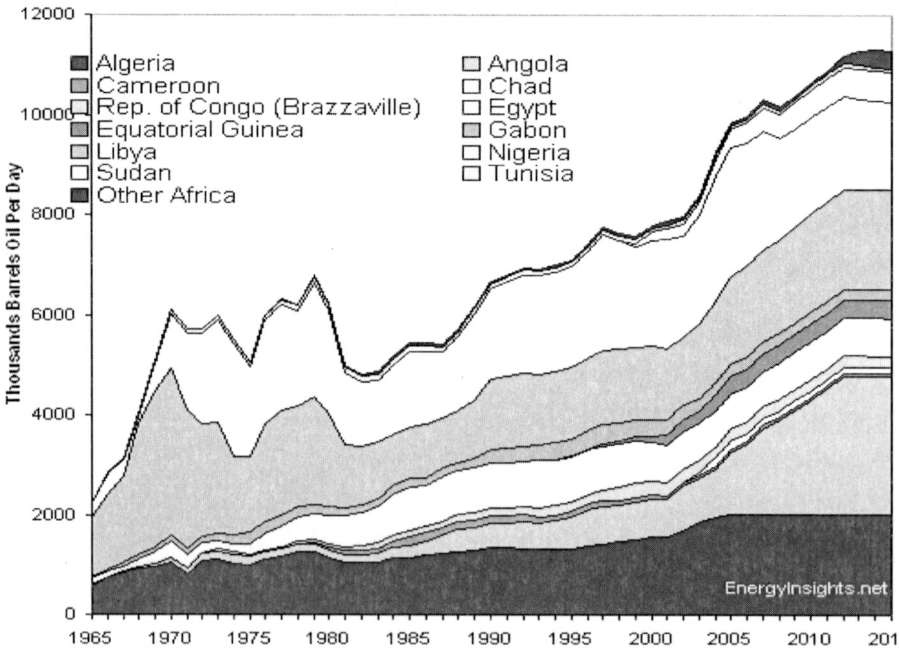

Source: Energy Insight.

Sub-Saharan Africa (SSA) produced nearly six million bbl/d of liquid fuels in 2012, i.e. about six percent of the total world oil production. Oil production in SSA has grown by an annual average of 36 percent over the past 10 years. Nigeria has been the top liquid fuels producer in the SSA region, followed by Angola. Together they accounted for 75 percent of total liquid fuels produced in Sub- Saharan Africa in 2012. Both these countries are expected to double their production by 2020. Sudan, which started exporting oil three years ago, now produces 1,86,000 barrels a day. However due to internal instability South Sudan has stopped production of oil.

The Gulf of Guinea, has large reserves of hydrocarbon energy resources. Eleven African countries such as Ivory Coast, Ghana, Benin, Togo, Nigeria, Cameroon, Gabon, Equatorial Guinea, Democratic Republic of Congo and Sao Tome and Principe share the same continental shelf. Among these Nigeria, Gabon, and Cameroon are major petroleum producers. The reserve is being estimated at 49.405 billion barrels and proven natural gas reserves are 194.975 Trillion Cubic Feet (TCF). This area is likely to become the world's leading deep water offshore production centre. Forty nine per cent of the total African oil production is concentrated in the Gulf of Guinea and this figure is predicted to rise up to 57 percent in 2030. With the opening of the Chad-Cameroon pipeline in July 2003, an estimated billion barrels of Chad's oil reserves can now find their way to the global market. Moreover, the geographical position of the Gulf of Guinea gives it an important comparative advantage for oil supply. Indeed, despite its relative proximity to the world's main consumers of energy, i.e. North America and Western Europe, the Gulf of Guinea benefits from the absence of narrow shipping maritime lanes, known as chokepoints, between the region and other parts of the world[4].

Moreover, Africa's oil and gas sectors are seeing continued growth with East Africa emerging as a new source of gas and oil. Large oil discoveries around Uganda's Lake Albert in 2006 and subsequent gas discoveries in offshore Mozambique have dramatically altered perceptions of East Africa. Uganda looks set to become one of the five largest oil producers on the continent, with its Lake Albert oil fields potentially capable of producing 200,000-350,000 barrels per day (bpd). Uganda's oil prospects are getting brighter after an additional one billion barrels of oil were recently announced as having been discovered, pushing the figures of commercially viable deposits up to at least 3.5 billion barrels. Mozambique is expected to become the second-largest exporter of LNG by 2025, as the country steps up production from 10 million tonnes per annum (Mtpa) in 2017 to an envisaged 50 Mtpa.

Fresh discoveries in neighbouring Kenya have boosted onshore exploration in that country and in March 2012, Kenya finally discovered oil after many years of exploration in the northern Turkana region. However, the reserves in that region have yet to be declared commercially viable. The director of the National Oil Corporation of Kenya (NOCK) concedes that, even if that were the case, production would not begin until 2018. Nonetheless, the signs are promising, with early indications suggesting that the Ngima-1 well in Turkana may hold reserves equivalent to those beneath Uganda's Lake Albert. Nevertheless, the country plays a vital role in the region as an oil transit hub, particularly for oil products coming into the region It should be noted that in 2008, Essar Energy Overseas, an Essar Oil subsidiary, signed an agreement to acquire a 50 percent stake in the Mombasa-based Kenya Petroleum. Meanwhile, there are hopes that both oil and gas could be discovered in Ethiopia in commercially viable quantities[5].

The oil fields in African continent are a magnet for investment and the competition for influence is fierce between European, US, Chinese, Indian and other Asian interests. Most oil producing countries in Africa are open to foreign investment, for exploration and production because they lack money, technology, skill and experts in these areas. Moreover, Africa's oil industries are not state controlled like Persian Gulf countries.

Presently, there are about 500 oil companies participating in the exploration and development of African oil field. Because of this investment, the total oil production in Africa is set to rise by 91 per cent between 2002 and 2025, from 8.6 to 16.4 million barrels per day according to US Department of Energy estimates. Malaquias suggests that foreign investors are attracted by the very competitive terms and conditions offered by African governments[6].

The "super" multinational corporations like Exxon-Mobil, Royal Dutch Shell, BP-Amoco-Arco, and Chevron-Texaco operate in Nigeria, Angola, Algeria, Congo-Brazzaville, Equatorial Guinea, Sao Tome and Principe, and Chad. In all these places they operate mostly in partnership with state oil corporations—in Nigeria's case, the Nigerian National Petroleum

Corporation; in Angola's case—with the Sociedad Nacional de Combustveis de Angola, Sonangol, and with the GNPC in Sudan.

Further, Asian multinational oil corporations (AMOC), like CNPC, CNOOC, and Sinopec from China and OVL from India are also undertaking vigorous business exploration in Africa. Highly competitive and strongly supported by the state, Chinese multinationals corporations are embarking on an acquisition drive and is capturing key resources and market share across Africa.

In terms of trade in oil, Africa has for years been seen by Western and Asian markets as an option for avoiding an almost total dependence on Middle Eastern oil. Robust demand from especially India and China over the past decade, fuelled by strong economic growth in these countries, has started to change not only Africa's export profile, but also the continent's economic landscape. Although Saudi Arabia is the principal supplier of oil to China, Angola occupies second place, with China importing nearly 9 per cent of its oil from Luanda, according to Trade Map figures. Other African countries that export to China include Congo (Brazzaville), Libya, Algeria, Equatorial Guinea, Nigeria, South Africa, Egypt. The Asian powerhouse is also an important trade partner of Sudan and South Sudan. Africa's oil exports to China are expected to increase, over the medium to the long-term, and the International Energy Agency projects that China will become the world's largest net importer of oil by 2020.

From the accompanying graphs, it is clear that both China and India are increasingly becoming the key destinations for Africa's oil exports. A review of the past few years, shows that whereas in 2007, 10 per cent of Africa's oil was shipped to China, and 5 per cent to India; by 2011, these figures had risen to 14 per cent and 8 per cent respectively. Oil contributes substantially to Africa's total export receipts; in 2011, an estimated 58 per cent of Africa's total export receipts, in value terms, derived from the category of 'mineral fuels, oils and distillation products'. In some individual countries, hydrocarbon exports account for over 95 per cent of export earnings.

Figure 4: Africa Oil Export Destination, 2011

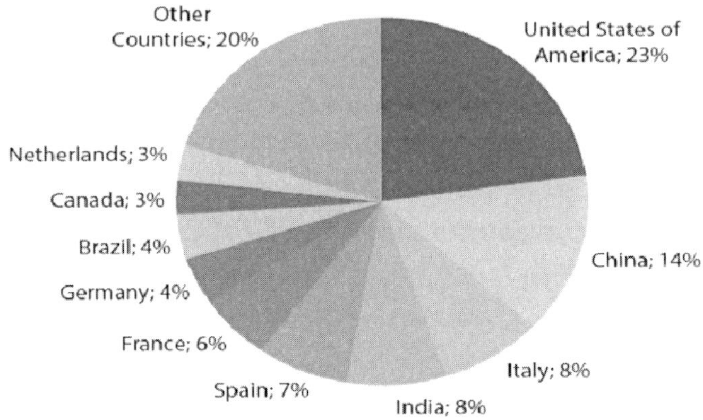

Source: Trade Map

According to a United Nations Conference on Trade and Development (UNCTAD) report FDI inflows to the region were mostly in extractive industries, such as oil, gas, and mining. Six oil producing countries Nigeria, Algeria, Chad, Egypt, Equatorial Guinea, and Sudan, accounted for about 48 percent of inflows to the region[7]. Uganda topped the East African region in attracting FDI, followed closely by Tanzania, on the back of increased investments in the oil and gas sector. As a result, inflows of investments to the region rose from $4.5 billion in 2011 to $6.3 billion in 2012. These inflows include Asian Foreign Direct Investment (FDI) which accounts for 10 percent of the total FDI in the world. For example, in 2011, Indian investment in Africa topped $ 2.5 billion[8].

It is noteworthy that in spite of the growing FDI, commodity boom, and natural resources, most of the oil rich African countries suffer from poor development, entrenched authoritarianism, political instability and violence. The prosperous sectors of the economy have no links with other sectors. The economy is incoherent because of the absence of backward and forward linkages. Moreover, some countries with the highest income inequality are oil producing states, such as Gabon, Nigeria, Angola, and Equatorial Guinea. In spite of the fact that fuel subsidies lead to inefficiencies and losses in the economy, local populations in countries like Nigeria, where 70 per cent of the population lives below the poverty line, view fuel subsidies as the only benefit of living in an oil-rich nation.

Several steps have been taken to diversify these economies but they have yielded mixed results[9].

India's Oil Diplomacy and Africa

India's engagement in Africa's oil fields is a recent phenomenon. Previously, India only had limited oil trade with Nigeria. It was only after the mid-1990s that India gradually began looking to Africa for its oil imports. India currently imports 20 percent of its oil from Africa, and has interests in all oil–rich African countries like Nigeria, Sudan, Republic of Congo and the West African States. However India has mostly focused on Nigeria and Sudan. It has invested $2 billion in the energy sector in Africa, with Nigeria being its leading supplier of oil. The Indian Oil Corporation (IOC) signed a term contract for one year with the Nigerian National Petroleum Corporation for importing 40,000 barrels of crude oil per day at the official selling price, to begin with.

It has been reported that India is also open to an aid-for-oil strategy and has already tried this strategy in Africa. In 2004, IOCL signed an MOU with the Edo state of Nigeria to build an oil refinery, in return for a stake in an oilfield in the state. The participation of OVL in Nigeria's upstream sector has forged significant energy ties between the two countries. It is of significance to note that India's energy engagement in the hydrocarbon sector is not only guided by economic and political factors, but certain ethical considerations have played an important role in directing engagement. Indian companies have initiated capacity building programmes in many of the countries. In Nigeria, for instance, ONGC has "not only carried out exploration and production successfully in very difficult terrains, but has also been responsive to the needs of local population in terms of development of healthcare facilities and education centres etc." Also "corporate social responsibility projects undertaken by ONGC in and around its project sites...have been immensely appreciated by the local community."[10] In 2005, Mittal Steel and ONGC announced an investment of $6 billion to establish a refinery, power plant and railway lines in Nigeria through a joint-venture company, ONGC-Mittal Energy Ltd (OMEL). As per this mega-deal between ONGC and the Nigerian government, OMEL would create the infrastructure, while Nigeria would give it oilfields.

In Sudan Indian presence grew when, in 1997, the US imposed comprehensive economic, trade, and financial sanctions against the country. The Sudanese government's military tactics also led US and western oil corporations withdrew from the field. Sudan, at that point of time was—internally ravaged by decades of civil war and externally isolated due to the extremist leaning of its military rulers. India quickly filled the vacuum[11]. Eventually, the Sudanese government renewed operations in the petroleum sector by striking partnerships with Asian oil companies. For instance, OVL bought shares of Canadian multinationals Talisman Energy in 2002. The Sudanese company, Sudapet Ltd., developed joint ventures with China National Petroleum Corporation (CNPC), India's Oil and Natural Gas Corporation (OVL), and Malaysia's Petronas[12].

India's investment in Sudanese oil fields proved controversial and debated in many academic and political forums all over India. At first, the debate mainly focused on the safety of OVL personnel rather than the morality of investing in a country with a dubious human rights record. The approval for the $720 million investment had many opponents. Some argued that committing hundreds of millions of dollars in a war-torn region was too risky and that OVL risked losing its investment[13]. The rationale for investing in a country ruled by a government that had harboured international terrorists was also questioned.

The Sudanese government backed the entry of OVL. While cooperation with China was considered important, they found it better to diversify their corporate and political partnerships to avoid being overly dependent on China. Thus the agreement with India was part of the Sudan government's broader foreign policy agenda. From India's perspective, while oil remains at the heart of the relationship and dominates Sudan's trade with India, the country has also been included in India's enlarged Focus Africa programme that was launched in 2002 to expand economic interaction with seven major trading partners. Besides oil, the government of India has identified five priority sectors, which are: infrastructure, agriculture, human resource development, information & communication technology, and small and medium industries. India has also extended an Export Import (EXIM) Bank Line of Credit of $50 million for the economic development of Sudan. To achieve this, the Indian Embassy in

Khartoum has formulated a Target and Introduce Programme (TIP) under which one new Indian product is introduced every semester.

India was undivided Sudan's third largest partner in the oil sector and its companies account for a 25 percent stake in its Greater Nile Oil Project which produces 280,000 bpd. The OVL completed a 741-km pipeline project from the Khartoum refinery to Port Sudan on the Red Sea, for transporting petroleum products for the Khartoum refinery. India made an initial investment of a billion dollars in the hydrocarbon sector, which was later increased to $ 2.5 billion. The OVL has stakes in several wells with a daily production of 160,000 barrels of which, 100,000 barrels per day are produced from wells that now fall within South Sudan. India used to get a million tonnes of crude oil per year from Sudan, which, in equity oil parlance, would mean a growth rate of 12 percent of the $750 million Indian investment. Incidentally, China is investing about $300 million to increase the capacity of the Khartoum refinery. However after independence, South Sudan closed down its oil production because of serious disputes relating to fees for transporting oil from South Sudan to Port Sudan on the Red Sea through Sudanese pipe-lines and the squabbles over the incomplete sections of the Comprehensive Partnership Agreement (CPA) between Sudan and South Sudan.[14]

In order to intensify oil diplomacy, India organised a two-day India-Africa Hydrocarbon Conference in New Delhi in the first week of November 2007. Oil ministers from 10 African countries, and delegations from 16 other countries participated in the conference and a road map was drawn up to identify the broad areas of cooperation in the hydrocarbon sectors between India and the African countries. India is keen to acquire more oil and gas fields as well as bag other energy projects, such as refineries, petrochemical plants and pipelines in Africa. Besides oil, India is also interested in importing liquefied natural gas (LNG) from Nigeria, Algeria and Egypt.

However, the Indian government and Indian oil companies are more concerned about the expanding Chinese presence in Africa[15]. The significant investments by China in the various sectors of the economies of African countries show that China is becoming a dominating factor in the region. It has been observed by many Indian academics that India has missed the bus in Africa despite its long association with the continent. The observation has been strengthened by the fact that Indian oil companies like ONGC lost out to their Chinese counterparts, who linked business with diplomacy to acquire oil and gas assets blocks in the new energy havens of West Africa. Increasingly, Chinese firms have also been outbidding OVL in the region. For instance, in Nigeria, in 2005, while OVL outbid CNOOC and acquired Nigeria's Akpo Field (OPL-246) from South Atlantic Petroleum Ltd, the Indian government rejected this acquisition on grounds of high political risk. Ultimately, CNOOC acquired OPL-246. In Uganda, ONGC lost out on acquisition of oil fields to China's CNOOC. According to a report, China's CNOOC has won the final production licence for Uganda's Kingfisher oil field and will spend $2 billion, over four years to develop it. Not only in Uganda, OVL has lost blocks in Angola as well as West Africa.

OVL's failure to achieve greater success is due in part to forces beyond its direct control. The government of India accords limited financial autonomy to OVL, and OVL must go through a lengthy approval process. OVL is empowered to invest on its own only in projects valued at less than $75 million. As a result, both international oil companies and African NOCs prefer Chinese NOCs as partners. The cash-rich Chinese companies, like CNPC, CNOOC, and Sinopec, in addition to leveraging the political, economic and diplomatic influence of the Chinese government, have also been bidding aggressively for oil producing properties.

By bidding higher, these companies are willing to accept lower rates of return, a price that China has so far been ready to pay for securing equity oil. Moreover, Chinese NOCs also have greater access to cheap capital than Indian oil companies, as they are able to borrow domestically at zero to one per cent interest rate (in comparison, the cost of capital in the domestic market for Indian SOEs and private sector enterprises is 10-11 per cent). Although finance is available at 3-4 per cent in the international market for very large sums, Indian companies are unable to tap into international finance owing to currency fluctuations and difficulties in getting collateral guarantees from banks, parent companies or even sovereign guarantees.

At present, OVL's operations do not enhance India's energy security to any great extent. OVL's unimpressive technical competence, especially in the international arena, severely limits its ability to acquire and manage promising acreage abroad. Most of OVL's manpower is drawn from ONGC, which has a poor performance record even in India, where it has been the main upstream player since the sixties. Further, ONGC has limited expertise in offshore exploration and virtually negligible experience in deepwater projects. So, in the present era of fiercely competitive bidding for promising prospects, it is doubtful whether OVL has the technical competence to assess the risk-reward scenarios well enough to gain any advantage. If it tries to stretch too far too quickly, it will be at extremely high financial risk; indeed, many of the exploration blocks acquired by OVL fall in the "very high risk" category.

Conclusion

The quest for energy security has prompted India's moves into the African oil sector. Given its major dependence on imported oil and its desire to diversify its oil supply sources, the country's foreign policy makers have been compelled to adopt a proactive policy towards Africa and to nurture its relations with major oil-producing African countries. In choosing to establish relations with African oil-producing countries, India enjoys the advantage of engaging with comparatively new oil producing countries in the Gulf of Guinea and Sudan, which also offer significant investment opportunities. It is also advantageous for India because there is limited competition in these countries.

On the other hand, African countries too are benefiting from India's engagement with them. Although investments in African countries are led by India's private sector companies, the government of India lends them its full support. Through its capacity-building programmes, India is one of the major players in infrastructure building (roads, railways, dams, power plants, etc.), pipeline projects, education and health in African countries. In fact, as discussed earlier, India's FDI in Africa has increased considerably.

India's capacity building programme is not without its flaws. In the case of Sudan, I noticed in my recent visit that there is only one clinic in Khartoum, raising the important question as to how effective is India's extensive Capacity Building program.

One of the significant challenges faced by Africa is that most of the foreign direct investment flowing into the continent is concentrated in the extractive industries. Other sectors have not benefited much, because there is practically no trickledown effect. As a result, the high growth rate of many African countries has not translated into meaningful economic structural transformation. In fact, there is hardly any job creation and poverty reduction, and this is compounded by a lack of transparency in financial governance. It cannot be overemphasised that the African countries that are benefiting from the rapid increase in world market prices for petrol and other raw materials need to prepare their respective economies for the future by diversifying their economies and making strategic investments. India can help these African countries to achieve long term development by recommending meaningful growth programmes and by supporting their efforts for improving their political and economic governance.

NOTES

1. Carl, J.; Rai, V. & Victor, D.G. 2008, 'Energy and India's Foreign Policy,' *Program on Energy and Sustainable Development*, Working Paper #75, at http://zunia.org/sites/default/files/media/node-files/ss/185331_SSRN-id1400184l262847047.pdf. (Accessed on 15 December 201).
2. Ibid.
3. Volman, D. 2006, *The Security Implications of Africa's New Status in Global Geopolitics*, African Security Research Project, Rutgers School of Art and Sciences,, at http://ruafrica.rutgers.edu/events/media/0809_media/volman_nai.doc (Accessed on 20 December 2013).
4. Price Waterhouse Coopers 2013, *From Promise to Performance: Africa Oil & Gas Review*, at http://www.pwc.co.za/en_ZA/za/assets/pdf/africa-oil-and-gas-review-2013.pdf. (Accessed on 15 December 2013).
5. Control Risks 2012, *A New Frontier: Oil and Gas in East Africa*, at http://www.controlrisks.com/OurThinking/CRsDocumentDownload/east_africa_whitepaper _LR_web.pdf. (Accessed on 15 December 2013).
6. Malaquais, A. 2005, 'Thirsty Powers: The United States, China, and Africa's Energy Resources', *Africa Center for Strategic Studies*, at http://africacenter.org/wp-content/uploads/2005/06/Thirsty-Powers-the-United-States-China-and-Africas-Energy-Resources.pdf. (Accessed on 15 December 2013).
7. UNCTAD World Investment Report 2013, *Global Value Chains: Investment and Trade for Development*, at http://unctad.org/en/publicationslibrary/wir2013_en.pdf. (Accessed on 15 December 2013).
8. Ibid, p. 7.
9. Obi, CI. 2009, 'Nigeria's Oil in Global Energy Security: Critical Issues and Challenges' in *Africa and Energy Security: Global Issues, Local Responses*, eds R. Beri & UK. Sinha, Academic Foundation, New Delhi pp. 128-134.

10. Ministry of Petroleum and Natural Gas 2009, *India and Nigeria discuss enhancing cooperation in oil sector*, Government of India, at http://pib.nic.in/release/rel_print_page1.asp?relid=46591. (Accessed on 12 December 2013).
11. n. 6.
12. n. 4.
13. Ibid.
14. BICC Brief #48 2013, *Oil Investment and Conflict in Upper Nile State, South Sudan*, at http://www.bicc.de/uploads/tx_bicctools/BICC_brief_48.pdf. (Accessed on 15 December 2013).
15. 'China's CNOOC to spend $2 bln on Uganda oil field', *The Africa Report*. 15 September 2013, at http://www.theafricareport.com/East-Horn-Africa/chinas-cnooc-to-spend-2-bln-on-uganda-oil-field.html. (Accessed on 15 December 2013).

11

Eliminating Energy Challenges in Nigeria to Guarantee Effective Supply of Oil and Gas to India in this Decade and Beyond

Alike Ambrose Ejiofor

Nigeria's Crude Oil Production

Nigeria's first recorded shipment of crude oil was from Shell's Oloibiri fields in 1958, which had an average production of 5,100 barrels per day. Today, according to the *Oil and Gas Journal*, Nigeria has crude oil reserves of 37.2 billion barrels. The daily production since August 2013 hovers between 2.2 million and 2.3 million barrels per day (bpd), according to the state-owned Nigerian National Petroleum Corporation (NNPC). An estimated 1.8 million barrels of the daily production consists of crude oil, condensates account for 400,000 to 500,000 barrels per day. Nigeria is the largest oil producer in Africa and the 11th largest in the world. Nigeria has four refineries with a combined capacity to refine 445,000 barrels per day. Two refineries with a combined capacity of 210,000 bpd are located in Port Harcourt, Rivers State; while the Kaduna State hosts the 110,000 bpd capacity refinery. The fourth refinery with a capacity of 125,000 barrels per day is located at Warri, Delta state. The United States Energy

Information Administration (EIA) estimates that only 280,000 barrels per day are refined by the four refineries, and are consumed locally. But even at the full capacity of 445,000 bpd, the four refineries can only produce about 10 million litres of Premium Motor Spirit (PMS), popularly known as petrol, while local consumption averages 35 million litres per day, according to the state-owned Petroleum Products Pricing Regulatory Agency (PPPRA). With the refineries operating sub-optimally the implication is that Nigeria depends on imports for 90 per cent of the petroleum products consumed locally.

Nigeria's Gas Production

Nigeria's proven gas reserves amount to 183 trillion cubic feet (tcf), an equivalent of 32 billion oil equivalent (boe), according to the Department of Petroleum Resources (DPR), which is the apex regulator for the oil and gas industry in Nigeria. Nigeria has the largest gas reserves in Africa and is the 9th largest global gas producer. With the country's unproven gas endowment is estimated at 600 trillion cubic feet by the EIA, the country is more of a gas nation rather than an oil nation. The gas produced in Nigeria consists of Associated Gas (AG), that is, gas produced with crude oil and Non-Associated Gas (NAG). According to DPR estimates, the country produces 5.20 billion Cubic Feet per day (bcf/d) of Associated Gas, while NAG accounts for 2.80 billion cubic feet per day, taking Nigeria's daily production capacity to 8.0 bcf/d. Of this, an estimated 6.6 bcf/d is for domestic consumption and export in the form of Liquefied Natural Gas (LNG). The balance 1.4 bcf/d is flared by the oil and gas producing companies operating in Nigeria. At the current price of $3.50 per 1,000 standard cubic feet of gas, the flared portion translates into a daily loss of $4.9 million in revenue—or $1.79 billion, annually. Currently, most of the gas produced is exported as Liquefied Natural Gas (LNG), by the Nigeria LNG Limited, located in the Bonny Island of Rivers State because the price of domestic gas does not guarantee adequate return on investment. The NLNG used to account for 10 per cent of global LNG supply but this has since dropped to seven per cent due to lack of investment in the expansion of capacity, that is required to sustain Nigeria's position. According to the NNPC, Nigeria's oil and gas industry has planned a $32 billion industry spend on gas development by 2020. It is estimated that if the country achieves this projection by 2017/2018, the combined production of gas in Nigeria would translate into the equivalent of 1.5 million barrels of oil equivalent per day. In fact, if the country achieves four to five billion cubic feet per day domestic utilisation of gas by 2018, Nigeria would be at par with South Korea in terms of domestic gas consumption, according to the NNPC estimates. Nigeria dominates the prolific Gulf of Guinea as Africa's largest oil and gas producer, with over one-fifth of the continent's crude oil and gas production. Thus any threat to energy supplies from Nigeria, would hugely impact the African output. The implication is that as India is becoming increasingly dependent on Africa, particularly Nigeria for crude oil, any major energy challenge in Nigeria will have grave consequences on India.

Threats Against Nigeria's Oil and Gas Development

The development of Nigeria's energy sector is currently hampered by the lack of infrastructure to harness the abundant gas resources; militancy; vandalism; crude oil theft; uncertainty in the operating environment as a result of the non-passage of the Petroleum Industry Bill (PIB); and the hostility of oil and gas-producing communities; among other factors.

Lack of Gas Infrastructure

With unproven gas reserves of over 600 trillion cubic feet, Nigeria has abundant gas resources, which in energy terms, are in excess of the 37.2 billion barrels of proven crude oil reserves. All the gas discoveries, so far, were made during crude oil exploration, and no deliberate efforts have been made to search for gas in Nigeria. In other words, there has been no focussed exploration of gas in Nigeria.

Nigeria's gas consists of Associated Gas (AG), that is, gas produced with crude oil, which accounts for about 63 per cent; and Non-Associated Gas (NAG), which is estimated at 37 per cent. Most of the gas produced in Nigeria is exported in liquefied form, through the Nigeria Liquefied Natural Gas (NLNG) Limited, while a large chunk of the AG is flared due to lack of infrastructure to harness the country's gas resources. The NLNG Limited used to account for 10 per cent of the global LNG supplies but due to various challenges facing Nigeria's gas development, other countries have overtaken Nigeria and the NLNG currently accounts for 7 per cent of global LNG supply. The country has plans to build two additional LNG plants—Brass LNG Limited on Brass Island in Bayelsa State and Olokola LNG, on the border between Ondo and Ogun States—but the international oil companies, which are the country's partners have not yet committed to supplying gas to the proposed plants. The Federal Government of Nigeria has initiated a Gas Master Plan to attract local and foreign investment to the tune of over $32 billion, for the development of the gas infrastructure in the country. However, the non-passage of the Petroleum Industry Bill (PIB) has made the operating environment unpredictable for investors. Some of these investors are relocating their investment to neighbouring countries such as Angola, Ghana and other oil and gas producing African countries, where the investment climate is predictable.

Militancy

Nigeria's oil and gas industry has for many years been attacked by militants from the oil-producing Niger Delta region of the country, who claim to be fighting against injustice and the long years of neglect of the oil-rich region. The attacks on oil workers and facilities started in 2005, when Nigeria was producing an average of 2.5 million barrels of crude oil per day. The militancy peaked in 2009, and crude oil production went down to 1.3 million barrels per day. This development prompted the late President Umaru Musa Yar'Adua to introduce an Amnesty Programme in 2009. Under the programme, militants were encouraged to surrender their weapons, without facing arrest or prosecution by the Nigerian government.

The militants, who surrendered are being imparted training and skills both in Nigeria and outside Nigeria. The amnesty programme, led to peace in the Niger Delta, and oil companies re-opened some of the oil fields that had been shut down during militancy. However, crude oil production in Nigeria is yet to reach the pre-militancy levels because not all the militants accepted amnesty. Some of the militants, who refused to surrender are still destroying oil and gas infrastructure. Some of the militants are however willing to surrender their weapons if the government would allow them to enjoy the benefits of the amnesty programme.

Crude Oil Theft/Vandalism

Barely three years after the amnesty programme, reduced destructive attacks on oil workers and facilities, creating conducive environment for oil companies to re-open the oil fields, Nigeria's crude oil production figures became very erratic, following several attacks on export pipelines by crude oil thieves.

Though destructive attacks on oil facilities and kidnappings of oil workers have reduced considerably in the Niger Delta, crude oil thefts and vandalism are on the rise. Crude oil thieves use hacksaws and other tools to perforate export pipelines and siphon off crude oil. Shell's major export lines in the eastern Niger Delta are the worst hit, forcing the company at one point, to shut-in 300,000 bpd because of this. The company has also had to resort to the *force majeure* clause with regard to crude oil shipments, as it can no longer fulfil its contractual obligations. The activities of oil thieves have threatened the capacity of the Nigerian government to implement the 2013 budget because oil revenues have been depleted. Shell, which is the largest producer in Nigeria, has said that it is losing 150,000 barrels per day to theft; while the Nigerian government has put the figure at 180,000 bpd. After siphoning off crude oil, these vandals let the oil spill into the environment, because they do not have the technology to repair the lines.

The Nigerian government had set a target of increasing the daily production to four million barrels per day; and the reserves to 40 billion barrels by 2010. But today, the daily crude oil production ranges between 2.2 million barrels to 2.3 million barrels per day because of the activities of crude oil thieves compared to the 2.5 million barrels per day recorded in 2005. Militancy and crude thefts have forced some international oil companies (IOCs) to start selling their onshore oil blocks to Nigerian indigenous companies, who know best how to manage the restiveness of the host communities.

The multinational companies are now focusing on deep-water operations that are more secure. Nigerian indigenous companies are currently celebrating the divestment exercises being carried out by the IOCs, as it will give them the opportunity of managing larger acreages. Shell is also said to be planning to put the Nembe Creek Trunkline (NCTL)—one of its two major export pipelines in the eastern Niger Delta—on sale. The old NCTL was replaced in 2010 at a cost of $1.1 billion but crude oil thieves perforated the new lines with hacksaws at over 200 points. Shell has sold several onshore blocks, while Chevron last week concluded the sale of three blocks, while another two have been put on sale.

Non-Passage of Petroleum Industry Bill (PIB)

Currently, there are about 17 laws regulating Nigeria's oil and gas industry some of which were promulgated over 50 years ago. Some of these include the Petroleum Profit Tax Act, 1959, which was amended in 1967, 1970, 1973 and 1979; the Mineral Oils (Safety) Regulations, 1963; Oil Pipeline Act 1956, as amended in 1965, after independence; Petroleum Act 1969 and the Petroleum (Drilling and Production) Regulations, 1969 with amendments in 1973, 1979, 1995, 1996 as well as Petroleum (Amendment) Decree 1996.

Others include the Nigerian National Oil Corporation (NNOC) Decree No 18 of 1971; Nigerian National Petroleum Corporation Decree 1977; Associated Gas Re-injection Decree 1979, as amended in 1985; Production Sharing Contract Decree of 1999 and the Petroleum Products Pricing Regulatory Agency (PPPRA) Act of 2003. These laws are obsolete and irrelevant for a modern oil and gas industry.

Since 2008, the Federal government has been working on the Petroleum Industry Bill (PIB), which is a single law that will replace the existing 17 laws. But the various controversial clauses in the PIB have made it difficult for the bill to be passed into law and this is creating anxiety among investors and uncertainty in the operating environment. Oil and gas investors have refused to take major investment decisions until the PIB is passed. Consequently, many deepwater projects, as well as gas projects running into billions of dollars have been put on hold. The multinational oil and companies are opposed to the fiscal provisions in the PIB because according to them, they are the harshest in the world.

The northern part of Nigeria, has no oil, but a majority of its population is opposed to certain provisions in the PIB because according to them the PIB is allocating too large a share of the oil revenue to the oil-producing Niger Delta.

The Senate and House of Representatives of Nigeria are opposed to certain provisions of the PIB because they give too much power to the minister of petroleum resources and too much discretion relating to the award of oil blocks to the President of Nigeria. The failure of the various stakeholders to reconcile their differences has led to the delay in the passage of the bill which has stalled major investments in Nigeria's oil and gas industry. These factors, coupled with the hostility of the oil-producing communities and the inability of the Nigerian National Petroleum Corporation (NNPC) to pay its cash calls to its joint venture partners, among others, have led to the stagnation in Nigeria's oil and gas industry.

Declining Exports to the United States

Nigeria is losing the United States as its biggest oil customer due to the country's increasing crude oil production and refinery closures in North America. Though this threatens the development of Nigeria's oil industry, it is a blessing for India as it will guarantee more exports to the country. One of the monthly data on the origins of crude oil imports released by the United States Energy Information Administration (EIA) has indicated that Nigeria was among the top five exporting countries that had accounted for 69 per cent of United States crude oil imports since January 2007. The country had consistently maintained its fifth position after Canada, Saudi Arabia, Mexico and Venezuela. According to the EIA, the United States crude oil imports from its top five foreign suppliers increased slightly during 2011, even though total United States crude imports fell to their lowest level in 12 years. As a result, the crude oil from these five countries accounted for a bigger share of overall United States crude oil imports, nearly 69 per cent, or just over 6.1 million barrels per day (bbl/d), said EIA.

The report noted that Canada, Saudi Arabia, Mexico, Venezuela, and Nigeria have consistently been America's five largest crude oil suppliers, although their rankings varied from year to year. However, United States purchases of crude oil in 2011 from Canada and Saudi Arabia went up while its imports from Mexico, Venezuela, and Nigeria declined, according to final trade data from EIA's February 2012, Company Level Imports report. Nigeria was also among the top ten countries that accounted for approximately 88 percent of all United States crude oil imports.

However, the situation has changed as United States crude oil production rose, and many refineries in North America, that refined Nigerian crude closed down. Citing data from the United States Energy Department, *Bloomberg News* reported that the US imports of Nigerian crude oil fell to a five-year low in February 2012, pushing the country from fifth to sixth position among suppliers to the world's largest oil consumer. The country's Nigerian oil imports fell to 352,000 barrels per day in February 2012, about a third of the amount purchased a year earlier, according to the Energy Department. To offset the trend, the Nigeria is sending crude oil cargoes to Asia twice the distance to the United States, according to data compiled by *Bloomberg.*

Possible Areas of Cooperation between India and Nigeria

International Campaign Against Crude Theft

India should join hands with Nigeria in the current efforts of President Goodluck Jonathan and the minister of petroleum resources, Ms Diezani Alison-Madueke to drum up the support of the international community against crude theft. The crude oil stolen in Nigeria is not refined in Nigeria but is shipped to foreign refineries on internationally registered vessels. There is no doubt that this illicit business would not thrive if the foreign refiners did not buy the stolen crude. India should use its influence to wage a global diplomatic campaign against this illicit business by lobbying the international community to ensure that foreign refineries do not buy crude oil from doubtful sources.

Joint Military Campaign Against Militancy/Crude Theft

As a world power, India should join other world powers to mount military surveillance in the Gulf of Guinea, particularly Nigeria's oil-producing Niger Delta to ward off vandals, crude oil thieves and militants. Exactly a month ago, a joint multi-national sea exercise, "African Winds," for ensuring a state of readiness to flush out crude oil thieves in the Nigerian waters was carried out in Lagos waters.

The military exercise, which was a part of the objective of the African Partnership Station (APS) aimed at stamping out maritime crime, was jointly carried out at the Takwa Bay Beach by Spain, United States, United Kingdom, the Netherlands and Nigeria. Aerial coverage of the exercise was provided by the Nigerian Navy Air Station, the US Marine Corps, Nigerian naval ships and special landing boats from the Netherlands. India can also contribute troops and military equipment to such exercises as part of its contribution to the effort.

Crude Oil Swap Arrangement

India can take advantage of Nigeria's inadequate refining capacity by supplying Nigeria with petroleum products in exchange for crude oil. Nigeria currently has crude oil swap arrangement with some foreign refiners. This arrangement is with the Nigerian National Petroleum Corporation (NNPC), which manages Nigeria's oil and gas assets for the Nigerian government.

Massive Inflow of Foreign Direct Investment/Participation of Indian Companies

The potential in Nigeria's oil and gas sector is enormous and offers abundant opportunities for investment. The Indian government should encourage investment in Nigeria's oil and gas sector. With the international oil companies (IOCs) selling their assets to Nigerian companies, Indian companies should be encouraged to build partnerships with Nigerian companies to harness these opportunities. There are abundant opportunities in Nigeria's gas sector as the sector is virtually untapped due to the concentration of efforts on oil.

Conclusion

It is expected that Nigerians will sort out the issue of PIB and enact a balanced petroleum law that will encourage investment and also enable Nigeria to benefit from its natural endowment. When the PIB is passed into law, host communities will be part-owners of oil and gas assets and this will guarantee security of the assets. With the decline in exports to the United States, there is no doubt that India will provide alternative market for Nigeria's oil. India and Nigeria have a lot to gain if they cooperate in the energy sector in view of Nigeria's great endowment, and the investment opportunities it offers in the sector.

12

Africa-India Uranium Commerce for Civil Nuclear Energy Cooperation

Rajiv Nayan

Introduction

Africa and India both need development, and for development, energy is indispensable. India is an energy deficient country, and is seeking energy from conventional and non-conventional sources. In October 2012, the then minister for petroleum and natural gas, S. Jaipal Reddy stated that, "India is likely to emerge as one of the top 3rd or 4th importers in the world, of all energy forms—oil, coal, gas and uranium."[1] India and Africa are in the process of developing multi-dimensional energy cooperation. Both the sides have made several achievements in energy cooperation, yet are exploring new areas for cooperation. Civil nuclear energy is one of the areas where cooperation in possible in the future.

Nuclear energy is an important element in India's potential energy mix. Although the Indian nuclear establishment has the long-term vision for increasing the nuclear energy component in the overall energy and electricity mix, the Nuclear Suppliers Group (NSG) highlighted India's need for civil nuclear energy at the global level. In fact, India is one of the primary drivers of the current phase of nuclear renaissance.

India's current nuclear expansion projects however requires uranium. Though India has relatively large reserves of thorium oxide[2], its uranium reserves are comparatively modest. As of October 2014, India has "established 2,14,158 t in-situ Uranium Oxide (U3O8) (1,81,606 tonne U) reserves, for indigenous production,"[3] and it regularly assesses the "techno-economic viability" of extracting and developing uranium resources. Not all uranium deposits are mined and processed. On various occasions, the mining and exploration of uranium reserves has been discontinued because it was not economically feasible.

The paper discusses the feasibility of the Africa-India Uranium Commerce for Civil Nuclear Energy Cooperation. India has an ambitious plan for civil nuclear energy expansion and Africa has uranium mines, though it is believed that China has bought most of the high-yield mines in several African countries. Notwithstanding China's aggressive purchase of mines, India can still gain access to uranium mines or at least uranium ores or similar products from Africa. However, the African-Indian uranium commerce has its share of challenges. Some of the challenges are political, some legal, some diplomatic and yet some others are economic and technical in nature. Quite naturally, different problems may need different solutions. Of all the challenges, the Pelindaba treaty appears to be the most worrying. This paper enumerates the various possible solutions for the supply of uranium from Africa for Indian nuclear energy programme. The paper briefly discusses India's civil nuclear energy plan and the potential of the African countries as natural uranium suppliers.

India's Civil Nuclear Energy Plan and the Need for Uranium

India has a three-stage nuclear power programme. However, the Indian government maintains that there is enough scope for the leading global nuclear energy countries and companies to enrich the energy mix of India. India has 18 operational Pressurized Heavy Water Reactors (PHWRs) of which: one plant has the capacity of 100 Megawatt electrical (MWe); one has 200 MWe capacity; 14 are of 220 MWe capacity; two plants have a 540 MWe capacity; along with four 700 MW PHWRs that are under construction. The much-awaited Kudankulam nuclear power plant-1 constructed in collaboration with Russia is the latest reactor to become operational. Kudankulam-2 is also expected to become operational soon;[4] each Kudankulam reactor has the capacity of 1000 MWe.

India is building six new nuclear reactors and has plans to build at least 25 more. The government of India has been frequently notifying its plans for the nuclear energy expansion. India's nuclear power capacity is expected to reach 10080 MW by 2017. India also has a plan to start work on 19 new nuclear power reactors by 2017.[5] If this plan materialises the country may have a total installed capacity of 17400 MW more in its energy basket. Earlier, India had planned to install about 20 GWe nuclear power plants by 2020;[6] and 274.56 GWe by 2052.[7] The plan may undergo some changes because of events like the Fukushima crisis.

According to the Department of Atomic Energy (DAE), as of March 2013:

> Out of 19 operating Nuclear Power Reactors in the country with installed capacity of 4680 MW, ten nuclear power reactors with a capacity of 2840 MW, are fuelled with indigenous uranium, which is not available in the required quantity. The remaining nine nuclear reactors with a capacity of 1840 MW are under International Atomic Energy Agency (IAEA) safeguards. These nine reactors use imported uranium, which is available in required quantity.[8]

However, in yet another statement, the DAE stated that imported uranium is being used in ten reactors under IAEA safeguards.[9]

The DAE has in the past accepted, that the shortage of uranium had affected the functioning of the power plants. Replying to a question in Parliament, the Indian government had stated that, "The country's uranium requirement in the 12th Five Year Plan [2012-2017] period is estimated to be 5057 tonnes. This includes 318 tonnes of low enriched uranium for Tarapur Atomic Power Station (TAPS)-1&2 and Kudankulam (KK)-1&2."[10] The Indian nuclear establishment maintains that India's known uranium deposits can feed nuclear power plants with a capacity of about 10,000 MWe only.[11]

India has agreements with various countries to procure uranium to fuel its increasing numbers of nuclear reactors. The Uranium Corporation of India Limited (UCIL) has been "exploring the possibility of participation in uranium properties with the companies"[12] in countries such as Namibia and Mongolia. Several countries such as Australia[13] and Canada[14] have signed agreements for supply of uranium to India. India is negotiating with these countries for detailed administrative/contractual agreements. As of now, India has purchased uranium from France, Russia, Kazakhstan[15], and Uzbekistan.[16] The Uzbek Company, M/s. NMMC Uzbekistan will supply 2000 MT of uranium in the form of uranium ore concentrate during 2014-2018.[17]

The government is also planning to "acquire stakes" in uranium mines in foreign countries.[18] Nuclear Power Corporation India Limited (NPCIL) and UCIL may form a joint venture company for the purpose[19] Indian companies may have partnership with Russia or any other country's entities to acquire stakes in uranium mines outside India. The government also intends to create a uranium reserve for the future.

Africa as a Supplier

African uranium is a major driver of the current nuclear energy renaissance in the world, though some refuse to accept it as the only reason. In fact, the argument is that African uranium was largely responsible for the very idea of a nuclear renaissance at the beginning of twentieth century when Belgium mined the uranium in 1915. African uranium enabled the nuclear weapon development in the United States. Between 1942 and 1944, the US purchased about 30, 000 metric tonnes of uranium from the Shinkolobwe mine in the Katanga province in the Democratic Republic of Congo.[20] This consignment enabled America to make first nuclear bomb. Africa got some bad publicity when A.Q. Khan came to be associated with its uranium. However, the allegation that African uranium was being used to manufacture an Iraqi nuclear weapon turned out be false.

Studies are indicating that Africa may emerge as an important supplier of uranium. It has substantial reasonably assured resources at its disposal. Three of the world's top 10 uranium mines are located in Africa—one in Niger and two in Namibia. In these countries, it is generally the foreign mining companies who operate the mines. However, several reports suggest that African companies are now trying to mine uranium with the help of 'local companies'.[21] Governments are investing in capacity-building to operate these mines. In the interim, the African governments may enact laws that make it mandatory for foreign companies "to educate, train and employ local staff in key positions in their African operations" as well as ensure "significant local shareholding".[22] The IAEA is also organising workshops and training programmes for the interested African countries so that these countries can develop an indigenous uranium industry.

Although South Africa is the only African member of the NSG, there are several other uranium producing countries in Africa. In 2012, for example, South Africa produced 465 metric tonnes of uranium, whereas Namibia and Niger each produced more than 4000 metric tonnes of uranium.[23] Malawi, which did not record any uranium production till 2008, mined 1101 metric tonnes of uranium production in 2012.[24] Four African countries account for about 20 percent of the global uranium production.[25] Moreover, Namibia and Niger are the largest producers of uranium through open-pit mining. Namibia has been increasing its production of uranium over the years. It is believed to possess five percent of the world's identified uranium resources.[26] In fact, although it has a very vibrant state-owned uranium company, but it has allowed the foreign companies to mine uranium.

Several other African countries are also exploring for uranium reserves through ongoing surveys and exploration. Algeria, Burundi, Congo, Ethiopia, Uganda are among the many other African countries that are supposed to have reasonable uranium reserves. Countries such as Botswana and Tanzania have uranium but it has not been mined for various economic and policy reasons. Some countries like Zambia produced limited amounts of uranium, but later had to stop production mainly for economic reasons. The location of increasing uranium reserves in Africa will certainly provide the uranium rich countries with more resources, which may be used for their overall development.

China, France, Japan, Russia, Spain, South Korea, Canada, Australia, and Russia are prominent countries that are interested in, or are already active in various uranium related activities. Some are active in exploration and mining, and some countries even use uranium for their power reactors. France imports about 80 per cent of the uranium used in its nuclear power plants from Africa. China, it seems, has purchased many uranium mines in Africa. China has been trying to get direct access to the global uranium supply. Its entry has been facilitated because of the low prices and the market slump because of the Fukushima incident.

China has signed several agreements with African countries. Niger, Algeria, and Namibia are some leading African countries with whom China has been developing a nuclear relationship. China and Niger are not only in talks for uranium mine development in the Niger but also for uranium trade.[27] China discussed the matter with Pan African Minerals regarding exploring Niger's uranium mining.[28] The China National Nuclear Corporation bought a 25 per cent stake in the Australian company—Paladin Energy Ltd—which is active in uranium mining in Africa in general and Namibia in particular.[29] This is not the first Chinese foray into Namibia. In 2012, China had invested in—the Husab project which is the world's biggest uranium mining project. The Chinese strategy apparently is to strongly influence uranium mining industry by developing a long-lasting business relationship with the African countries.[30]

All African countries are the members of the Non-Proliferation Treaty (NPT). All the key uranium producing or uranium possessing countries have joined the Convention on the Physical Protection of Nuclear Material (CPPNM) and some of them have even ratified the 2005 Amendment. The main countries, which have joined the CPPNM, are Algeria, Central African Republic, Malawi, Niger, Nigeria and South Africa. Of them Algeria, Niger and Nigeria have already ratified the Amendment. These countries are also engaged with the United Nations Security Council Resolution 1540 implementation programmes. Most of the relevant countries have the required legislative and regulatory mechanisms to enforce nuclear safety and security requirements. Wherever there are gaps, the international community and regional organisations like the Africa Union assist them in plugging them. However, a section of the non-proliferation community is making some unrealistic safeguards related demands. These expectations are not in congruence with international practices.

Challenges

However, these countries may have to overcome some challenges to sell their uranium in the world market. First, rebels in some of these countries, cause problems in mining areas. France had to send Special Forces to deal with the rebels in Niger. Second is the insufficient technical and economic capacity of these countries, for undertaking exploration and mining work. Third is the current low price of uranium, because of the Fukushima incident. Fourth is the regulatory issue. Many of the countries interested in uranium mining and selling may have to put in place elaborate legal, regulatory and enforcement frameworks.

More importantly, the Pelindaba treaty that establishes the African Nuclear-Weapon-Free Zone was signed on April 11, 1996 and entered into force in 2009. The member countries may have to decide on Article 9 (c) of the treaty that makes it mandatory for them:

> Not to provide source or special fissionable material, or equipment or material especially designed or prepared for the processing, use or production of special fissionable material for peaceful purposes to any non-nuclear-weapon State unless subject to a comprehensive safeguards agreement concluded with IAEA.

After the 2008 NSG exemptions, India signed agreements and contracts with several countries for the supply of uranium. So far, it has received uranium from three countries, namely, France, Russia and Kazakhstan but India wants to diversify its uranium supply. It has therefore signed agreements with countries such as Mongolia and Canada for the supply of uranium.

But India also wants uranium from Africa and thus has signed a uranium agreement with Namibia as well. This agreement, officially known as the 'Agreement between the Government of the Republic of India and the Government of the Republic of Namibia on Cooperation in Peaceful Uses of Nuclear Energy,'[31] was signed on August 31, 2009. Later, a DAE delegation visited Namibia from May 18-21 2011, for the commercial operationalisation of the agreement and a protocol for the supply of 168 metric tonnes of uranium ore, was signed by the two countries.[32] As Namibia is yet to ratify the 2009 bilateral agreement, no further steps for the delivery of the uranium have been taken.

Other countries in Africa have also been expressing an interest in doing business with India. South Africa, the only NSG country, after some initial hesitation agreed to the idea of selling uranium to India. The Tanzanian

Prime Minister Pinda wanted a 'real friend' like India to invest in uranium mining. Uganda wants India to access its uranium reserves and for this, it wants India to train its engineers. The minister of finance planning and economic planning in Uganda led a delegation to the Confederation of Indian Industry and asked Indian companies to help develop the uranium sector in his country—among other requests. Similarly, other countries such as Malawi, Burundi, Congo, Mali, and Gabon are also interested in entering onto uranium commerce with India and said so officially and publicly.

The African academic and policy communities are discussing the ways and means for overcoming the challenges that are coming in the way of doing uranium business with India. The most important, and to an extent the real obstacle is the Pelindaba Treaty. Article 19 of the treaty lays down:

1. Any amendments to the Treaty proposed by a Party shall be submitted to the Commission, which shall circulate it to all Parties.
2. Decision on the adoption of such an amendment shall be taken by a two-thirds majority of the Parties either through written communication to the Commission or through a conference of Parties convened upon the concurrence of a simple majority.
3. An amendment so adopted shall enter into force for all parties after receipt by the Depository of the instrument of ratification by the majority of Parties.

Currently, there are 39 state parties, though there are 50 signatories. It means that the consent of 26 countries is required, for the NSG kind of India-specific exemptions. India should not have any difficulty in giving the same undertaking that it gave to the NSG member countries,[33] and before that to the US. India can give "long-standing and steadfast commitment to universal, non-discriminatory and total elimination of nuclear weapons". It may also reiterate other relevant pledges such as: strengthening the international non-proliferation regime; not subscribing to any arms race, including a nuclear arms race; concluding a universal, non-discriminatory and verifiable multilateral Fissile Material Cut-off Treaty in the Conference on Disarmament; and exercising a tighter control on the source of proliferation of sensitive technologies, including enrichment and reprocessing transfers.

India has signed a comprehensive umbrella safeguards agreement with the IAEA in 2008. The agreement covers: nuclear material along with nuclear facilities; non-nuclear material; equipment; components; special fissile material generated with the help of safeguarded facilities or goods; heavy water and so on. The general principle of the agreement is to ensure that safeguarded nuclear material is not withdrawn or transferred, whenever and wherever India wants. It has to follow certain procedures.

Certainly, India will not use uranium for weapons or any other military purposes. Under this agreement, a previously concluded safeguards agreement may continue, if all parties give their consent.

Under the new agreement, imported uranium is to be used in a facility that is under safeguards. Such facilities are to be notified to the IAEA by India. The import of uranium is to be notified within four weeks of its arrival. India also has to inform the IAEA about all the facilities that are using imported uranium, and the precise amount of uranium in each nuclear facility. If any uranium—under safeguards- is to be transferred to any other facility, India has to inform about that reactor to the IAEA. Section E of the agreement has provisions for conversion plants, enrichment plants and fabrication plants. Special procedures have been laid down for reports, inspections, residues, scrap and waste and blending of nuclear materials at these sites.

So far, India has signed international safeguards with only one inspection agency—the IAEA. Before July 18, 2005, it had already signed agreements with the IAEA to put six reactors under safeguards. All these reactors were placed under the provisions of the IAEA document INFIRCIRC/66/Rev.2. Moreover, India had accepted facility-specific safeguards for those installations. Nevertheless, when the July 18, 2005 India-US joint statement proposed to separate India's nuclear facilities into civilian and military/ strategic, it agreed to place several of its other facilities under IAEA safeguards.[34]

As stated above, India has already signed agreements with NSG member countries such as France, Kazakhstan and Canada for the import of uranium. It is at an advanced stage of negotiations with Australia for supply of uranium. All these agreements have already addressed diversion and proliferation related issues. These agreements could fulfil the non-proliferation requirements of the Pelindaba treaty and reassure its member countries.

Moreover, the nuclear establishment has control mechanisms that derive their principal statutory authority from the Atomic Energy Act of 1962 which has since been amended a few times. India regulates its uranium with a range of laws, rules, codes and directives. These controlling regulatory mechanisms have evolved over the years. India also has strong physical protection legal and regulatory frameworks in place along with strict security codes and guidelines for transportation of uranium. The Indian government undertakes its own threat perception exercises through its specialised agencies and departments. The threat perception or "Design Basis Threat" guides nuclear security preparedness. Although India does not export uranium, yet it has a comprehensive export control framework in place for the purpose.

Conclusion

There are conflict zones and rebellions in Africa. These conflicts are highlighted as challenges or stumbling blocks in the way of uranium mining. Such conflicts have existed at one time or the other in other parts of the world as well. The concerned parties have resolved conflicts through innovation and various other mechanisms. These mechanisms have often been supported by economic development. No doubt, the money accruing from the sale of uranium will be useful for economic development in these conflict zones, which in turn may lead to peace and stability in the region. So, uranium commerce will take place under the peace and security framework that the Pelindaba treaty wants to establish in the African region.

Most major African countries have either adequate legal, regulatory and institutional frameworks in place to implement the treaties and global best practices. The countries, which lack such a framework, are generally not resistant to adopting the framework. These countries are participating and interacting bilaterally, regionally and globally at different forums to strengthen their nuclear governance facilities. However, it would be unfair to expect them to implement an unequal or unrealistic agreement or treaty. Any idea or treaty needs to be contextualised. There must be a balance. NSG exemptions have been made for India, and the participant countries, mainly from the developed world are signing all kinds of bilateral treaties with India It would be unjust if African countries are denied an access to the Indian market.

For sure, cooperation between India and Africa on uranium commerce may mark a new beginning. It may have an impact on other sectors as well. India and Africa will both gain from this. India may share its mining experience with African countries, and these countries that are seeking to develop their own mining companies will benefit immensely from this. India and African countries can even enter into joint ventures to explore and mine uranium. More importantly, some African countries are willing to build their own nuclear power plants, and India's help in this which would be less expensive for them. India can offer a range of reactors from 200 MW to 700 MW, or may be more in the future, which will give these African countries a choice.

NOTES

1. Government of India, Ministry of Petroleum and Natural Gas, "Need Proactive Action on three Fronts for Ensuring Energy Security: Shri S. Jaipal Reddy", Press Information Bureau, October 15, 2012, http://pib.nic.in/newsite/mbErel.aspx?relid=88403 (Accessed on October 12)
2. 8.56 lakh tonnes of thorium oxide as per Government of India, Department of Atomic Energy, Lok Sabha, starred Question No 379, "Untapped Uranium/Thorium Reserves" December 19, 2012, http://dae.nic.in/writereaddata/lssq%20379.pdf (Accessed on October 12, 2013)
3. Government of India, Department of Atomic Energy, Lok Sabha, Unstarred Question No 282, "Changes in Atomic Energy Policy", December 10, 2014, http://dae.nic.in/writereaddata/lsus2821.pdf (Accessed on October 12, 2013)
4. Nuclear Power Corporation of India Limited, "Kudankulam Atomic Power Project", at http://www.npcil.nic.in/main/ConstructionDetail.aspx?ReactorID=77 (Accessed on October 12, 2013)
5. Government of India, Department of Atomic Energy, Lok Sabha, Unstarred Question No 643, "Nuclear Power Generation", February 27, 2013, http://dae.nic.in/writereaddata/parl/bud2013/lsus643.pdf (Accessed on October 12, 2013)
6. Government of India, Department of Atomic Energy, "Meeting Demand Projection," http://dae.nic.in/?q=node/129 (Accessed on October 12, 2013)
7. Government of India, Department of Atomic Energy, Tables, http://dae.nic.in/?q=node/133 (Accessed on October 12, 2013)
8. Government of India, Department of Atomic Energy, Lok Sabha, Unstarred Question No 3692, "Shortage of Uranium", March 20, 2013, at http://dae.nic.in/writereaddata/parl/bud2013/lsus3692.pdf (Accessed on October 12, 2013)
9. Government of India, Department of Atomic Energy, Lok Sabha, Unstarred Question No 3601, "Uranium Reserves", August 24, 2011, at http://dae.nic.in/writereaddata/3601_lsus240811.pdf (Accessed on October 12, 2013)

10. Government of India, Department of Atomic Energy, Lok Sabha, Unstarred Question No 396, "Requirement of Uranium", December 21, 2012, http://dae.nic.in/writereaddata/lssq396_211211.pdf (Accessed on October 12, 2013)
11. Government of India, Department of Atomic Energy, Lok Sabha, Unstarred Question No 3278, "Uranium Reserves", December 14, 2011, http://dae.nic.in/writereaddata/3278-lsus141211.pdf (Accessed on October 12, 2013)
12. Government of India, Ministry of Atomic Energy, Lok Sabha, Acquisition of Uranium Mines Abroad, Unstarred Question no 3547, answered on July 29, 2009, (Accessed on October 12, 2013)
13. Government of India, Ministry of External Affairs, "Joint Statement on the State Visit of Prime Minister of Australia to India", September 5, 2014 at http://www.mea.gov.in/bilateral-documents.htm?dtl/23976/Joint+Statement+on+the+State+Visit+of+Prime+Minister+of+Australia+to+India; Accessed on January 31, 2015; Government of India, Ministry of External Affairs, "MOUs/Agreements signed during the visit of Prime Minister of Australia to India (September 4-5, 2014)", September 5, 2014, at http://www.mea.gov.in/bilateral-documents.htm?dtl/23975/MOUsAgreements+ signed+during+the+visit+of+Prime+Minister+of+Australia+to+India+45+September+2014 (Accessed on January 31, 2015)
14. Government of India, Ministry of External Affairs, "Note on Agreement and MOUs signed with Canada during PM's visit", June 27, 2010, at http://www.mea.gov.in/media-briefings.htm?dtl/2989/Note+on+Agreement+and+MOUs+signed+with+ Canada+ during+PMs+visit; Prime Minister of Canada Office, "Canada-India Nuclear Cooperation Agreement", http://www.pm.gc.ca/eng/news/2012/11/06/canada-india-nuclear-cooperation-agreement (Accessed on October 12, 2013)
15. Government of India, Department of Atomic Energy, Lok Sabha, Unstarred Question No 3692, "Shortage of Uranium", March 20, 2013, at http://dae.nic.in/writereaddata/parl/bud2013/lsus3692.pdf (Accessed on October 12, 2013)
16. Government of India, Department of Atomic Energy, Lok Sabha, Unstarred Question No. 4894, "Agreement for Supply of Uranium", August 13, 2014 at http://dae.nic.in/writereaddata/parl/budget2014_2/lsus4894.pdf (Accessed on October 12, 2013)
17. Ibid.
18. Government of India, Department of Atomic Energy, Lok Sabha, Unstarred Question No 378, "Shortage of Uranium", March 14, 2012, at http://dae.nic.in/writereaddata/lsus378.pdf (Accessed on October 12, 2013)
19. Government of India, Department of Atomic Energy, Rajya Sabha, Unstarred Question No 1246, "New Uranium Mines in the Country", August 23, 2012, http://dae.nic.in/writereaddata/rsus1246.pdf (Accessed on January 31, 2015)
20. Nicolas Dasnois, "Uranium Mining in Africa: A Continent at the Centre of a Global Nuclear Renaissance", *SAIIA Occasional Paper* Number 122, September 2012, p.5.
21. Ian Anthony and Lina Grip, "Africa and the Global Market in Natural Uranium: From Proliferation Risk to Non-proliferation Opportunity", *SIPRI Policy Paper 39*, November 2013, http://books.sipri.org/files/PP/SIPRIPP39.pdf (Accessed on October 12, 2013)
22. Ibid
23. World Nuclear Association, "Uranium Production figures: 2002-2012", July 2013, http://www.world-nuclear.org/info/Facts-and-Figures/Uranium-production-figures/ (Accessed on January 31, 2015)
24. Ibid
25. International Atomic Energy Agency, "Uranium Mining in Africa: Gathering Momentum",

May 4, 2012, http://www.iaea.org/OurWork/ST/NE/NEFW/News/2012/repository/Uranium-mining-in-africa.html (Accessed on January 31, 2015)

26. World Nuclear Association, "Uranium in Namibia", September 2014, http://www.world-nuclear.org/info/Country-Profiles/Countries-G-N/Namibia/ (Accessed on January 31, 2015)
27. China National Nuclear Corporation, "Sun Qin Met with Mr. Tchiana, the Minister of Mine of Niger", February 20, 2014, http://www.cnnc.com.cn/tabid/655/InfoID/80262/frtid/645/Default.aspx (Accessed on January 31, 2015
28. China National Nuclear Corporation, "Cao Shudong Met With Frank Timis, Chairman of Pan African Minerals", February 18, 2014, http://www.cnnc.com.cn/tabid/655/InfoID/80185/frtid/645/Default.aspx (Accessed on January 31, 2015)
29. "Deals of the day- Mergers and acquisitions", *Reuters,* Jan. 20, 2014, http://www.reuters.com/article/2014/01/20/deals-day-idUSL3N0KU2RE20140120 (Accessed on January 31, 2015)
30. Lyu Chang, CNNC buying stake in Namibia uranium mine, *China Daily* (Europe), January 21, 2014, http://europe.chinadaily.com.cn/business/2014-01/21/content_17248169. htm (Accessed on January 31, 2015)
31. Government of India, Department of Atomic Energy, Lok Sabha, Unstarred Question No 1116, "Civil Nuclear Agreement," March 3, 2010, http://dae.nic.in/writereaddata/lsus030310.pdf#page=10 (Accessed on January 31, 2015)
32. Government of India, High Commission of India, "India-Namibian Bilateral Relations," October 1, 2013, http://www.highcommissionofindia.web.na/Downloads/Bilateral%20 Relations.pdf (Accessed on January 31, 2015)
33. Government of India, Ministry of External Affairs, "Statement by External Affairs Minister of India Shri Pranab Mukherjee on the Civil Nuclear Initiative", September 5, 2008 http://www.mea.gov.in/in-focus-article.htm?18806/Statement+by+External+Affairs+Minister+of+India+Shri+Pranab+Mukherjee+on+the+Civil+Nuclear+Initiative (Accessed on January 31, 2015)
34. International Atomic Energy Agency, "Agreement between the Government of India and the International Atomic Energy Agency for the Application of Safeguards to Civilian Nuclear Facilities: Addition to the List of Facilities Subject to Safeguards Under the Agreement", INFCIRC/754/Add.1, November 12, 2009, http://www.iaea.org/Publications/Documents/Infcircs/2009/infcirc754a1.pdf (Accessed on January 31, 2015); International Atomic Energy Agency, "Agreement between the Government of India and the International Atomic Energy Agency for the Application of Safeguards to Civilian Nuclear Facilities: Addition to the List of Facilities Subject to Safeguards Under the Agreement", INFCIRC/ /754/Add.2, April 7, 2010, http://www.iaea.org/Publications/Documents/Infcircs/2010/infcirc754a2.pdf; (Accessed on January 31, 2015); International Atomic Energy Agency, "Agreement between the Government of India and the International Atomic Energy Agency for the Application of Safeguards to Civilian Nuclear Facilities: Addition to the List of Facilities Subject to Safeguards Under the Agreement", INFCIRC/ /754/Add.3, December 16, 2010, http://www.iaea.org/Publications/Documents/Infcircs/2010/infcirc754a3.pdf; (Accessed on January 31, 2015); International Atomic Energy Agency, "Agreement between the Government of India and the International Atomic Energy Agency for the Application of Safeguards to Civilian Nuclear Facilities: Addition to the List of Facilities Subject to Safeguards Under the Agreement", INFCIRC/ /754/ Add.4, December 19, 2012, http://www.iaea.org/Publications/Documents/Infcircs/2012/infcirc754a4.pdf (Accessed on January 31, 2015).

Index